THE
Conversion
CODE

THE
Conversion
CODE

CAPTURE INTERNET **LEADS**

CREATE QUALITY **APPOINTMENTS**

CLOSE MORE **SALES**

CHRIS SMITH

WILEY

For general information about our other products and services, please contact our Customer Care Department within the United States at (800) 762-2974, outside the United States at (317) 572-3993 or fax (317) 572-4002.

Wiley publishes in a variety of print and electronic formats and by print-on-demand. Some material included with standard print versions of this book may not be included in e-books or in print-on-demand. If this book refers to media such as a CD or DVD that is not included in the version you purchased, you may download this material at http://booksupport.wiley.com. For more information about Wiley products, visit www.wiley.com.

Library of Congress Cataloging-in-Publication Data is available.

ISBN 978-1-119-21188-4 (hardback)
978-1-119-21189-1 (epdf)
978-1-119-21190-7 (epub)

Cover image: Mike Mangigian
Cover design: Wiley
Internal Graphics & Charts: Mike Mangigian and Allie DeCastro
Edited by: Steve Smith

Printed in the United States of America

10 9 8 7

Contents

Introduction: How The Conversion Code Was Created

The Conversion Code is a new blueprint for marketers and salespeople that shows you how to capture and convert Internet leads into closed sales at the highest rate possible. Using my exact "code" outlined in this book, you will immediately get more website traffic and more Internet leads, but, most importantly, close more sales.

During the last decade, I worked inside sales jobs and have called more than ten thousand Internet leads. I even worked for two different billionaires: Dan Gilbert and Lou Pearlman. Gilbert is most notably the owner of Quicken Loans and the Cleveland Cavaliers, while Pearlman sadly/impressively made household names of Britney Spears, *NSync, and the Backstreet Boys. I've got a decent three-point shot and I love to sing in the shower, but they didn't hire me for those skills. Instead, I was an elite-level inside salesperson for their ten-figure organizations.

At Quicken Loans for Gilbert, I sold mortgages (when interest rates were over 7 percent and the housing market was crashing). At Fashion Rock, for Pearlman, I sold "event vacations" in Orlando, where talent agents were (sort of) looking for the next big thing. Like a pre-*American Idol*, *American Idol*.

At both companies, I sold over the phone from a cubicle (dialing for dollars *Boiler Room*–style), calling people who had requested more information online (or through a radio or TV ad). I was given a name, a number, and a phone. My job was to call the leads and close them, that day, including getting their credit card number. For the loans, I also had to get a contract signed and get the lead to give me their Social Security number over the phone within the first five minutes of the call.

In *The Conversion Code* I will teach you exactly what, when, and how to say things over the phone to people so that day in and day out you convince them to buy from you. In fact, the sales script in Section Three of this book works so well and is so easy for you to duplicate that it should almost be illegal (spoiler alert: some of what I learned at Lou Perlman's company actually was).

You will indeed feel like what you are learning in this book gives you an unfair advantage. It does. I often stop as I am teaching the "code" to remind myself that while it does feel amazing to be so good at inside sales that you can quite literally sell anyone anything, you also need a Spider-Man mentality: With great power comes great responsibility.

Taking what I learned doing inside sales (the legal and ethical parts) for Gilbert and Pearlman, I landed an outside sales job that included selling from the stage as a keynote speaker for Move Inc. Move is a publicly traded company now owned by NewsCorp (Rupert Murdoch's Fox News/Wall Street Journal empire) and is nearly a billion-dollar market cap company. To start, I drove to two offices each day throughout the state of Florida and sold CRM, websites, and other online marketing solutions to real estate agents. I had to leave the office with a signed contract or the sale went to the inside sales team and I didn't get the commission. I also spoke at national trade shows and conferences, again having to close that day or not getting a commission. Using my "code," I won Move's Presidents Club Award in my first year, outselling their most seasoned reps, even though I had no experience in outside sales OR selling software.

It was during my time at Move when I started video blogging and using Facebook for business purposes under a brand I co-founded for them (with an amazing guy named Steve Pacinelli) called Tech Savvy Agent. Within no time we were getting 100,000+ page views per month and generating tens of thousands of Likes and Leads. Basically, I had only been a salesperson my entire life until I started Tech Savvy Agent. Now, I was a marketer too. And the leads I was generating were quality and they were closing . . . .

Next, I was hired to be a sales coach and public speaker for the inside and outside sales teams at DotLoop, a transaction management and electronic signature company. My official job title was actually "Chief Paper Killer." As I taught DotLoop's sales team "The Conversion Code" you could see the lightbulbs going off. They left every sales coaching session lusting to get back on the phones. They would show up telling me they "just needed help closing" and they would leave telling me that my "code" was their "best sales coaching ever" and an immediate "game changer." During my third year with the company, DotLoop was acquired for $108 million by Zillow Group. Not quite another billion dollar experience, but a nine-figure exit is not too shabby.

Today, I am a partner at my own company—Curaytor. Curaytor specializes in helping small business owners with lead generation and lead conversion through our simple software and proven strategies. We combine ideas and innovation with execution for small business owners who are too busy to do everything themselves. Each and every month we generate tens of thousands of Internet leads, turning many of them into closed sales. Simply put, we do "The Conversion Code" that you will learn in this book for them (minus calling their leads, for that we give them the script that is in Section Three).

Here are a few testimonials from our clients at Curaytor:

"Before using Curaytor I was at about $200k (in income). Looks like my next 12 months may be in the $600–$750k range."

"In the 1st 6 months of 2015 we bypassed our 2014 Total Sales!"

"I have doubled my business"

"Business increased by over 100% in 12 months"

"2015 will be our best year ever"

"Best investment I've made in my 14 years...Hands down."

"My business is up 52% since we partnered with Curaytor and we are looking at growing another 50% next year!"

Using "The Conversion Code," for ourselves Curaytor passed $5,000,000 in annual recurring revenue in less than three years (and we are growing like a weed). To ensure the success of my first start-up, I even personally got back on the phone and sold the first couple million in recurring revenue myself, using the exact strategies and scripts that are in this book.

The only difference between doing inside sales for yourself and doing it for someone else is that you need (a) something awesome to sell that you own and (b) qualified leads to sell it to. So in the first two sections of *The Conversion Code*, I will teach you exactly how we generate great Internet leads (at a low cost per click, lead, and acquisition) and how we use technology, people, and marketing automation to turn those leads into an endless supply of quality appointments for our sales team.

With that being said, I truly believe marketing automation is greatly overrated and is being used too frequently as a crutch. Technology and software have become an excuse not to do the real work of picking up the phone and talking to people about what you sell and whether it is right for them. If you want to make more money by closing online leads, you have to pick up the damn phone. If you have more usernames and passwords than customers you are doing it wrong.

The idea of a "cart" or "e-commerce" is a myth for most. Sure, we may buy things from Amazon or Zappos without ever speaking to a sales rep, but if YOU actually think that YOU can simply get leads from the Internet to buy stuff from YOU (that actually costs more than a few dollars) without ever calling them, YOU are wrong. Bottom line? Most companies need to pick up the phone to close a lead and are so focused on working smarter, not harder, that they are tripping over nickels to pick up pennies. Never forget that conversations create closings.

I feel really blessed that I learned how to sell before I learned how to market. I learned how to convert leads before I learned how to generate them. So when I became a marketer, I saw a big responsibility in my new role. My approach to marketing came from my work in the inside sales cubicle, knowing from first-hand experience how difficult it can be to dial for dollars every single day. How could I approach marketing wanting to get bad leads just so that I could point to vanity metrics that don't even matter? I know my sales script works, and I respect a salesperson's time because I am one, so when I teach you how to generate leads be rest assured that my goals are quantity AND quality.

Marketing can do a much better job of sending purchase-ready leads to sales. In fact, if most marketers actually had to call the leads they're generating, they'd want to quit their job or fire themselves. It's one thing to get someone to "Like," "Follow," or subscribe by email—it's another to get their time. And it's a whole other thing to get someone's credit card number.

Due to the recent digital revolution I will even go as far as to proclaim that every lead is now an Internet lead. We're all online, every day all day. The world is changing, and your strategies need to change along with it. We look at Facebook on our phones more than we look at each other in the face. Regardless of whether they submit their information through the web form on your website or not, every human is now conditioned to look online before making a purchase. And thanks to our social media addiction you can now generate demand, not just fulfill it.

If you are in sales or marketing and your job doesn't involve Internet leads, then I have some bad news for you: You're really missing out and leaving tons of money on the table. I have good news for you, too: You picked up this book. Whether you're in marketing or sales, whether you're a seasoned sales rep or new to social media marketing, *The Conversion Code* is your guide to getting an ROI, ASAP.

How to Crack The Conversion Code

WHAT IS THE CONVERSION CODE?

The Conversion Code is the new formula for being a great marketer and salesperson in the Internet era. It's a proven step-by-step blueprint to increasing leads and sales, immediately. Today's customers are savvy, and they have more options than ever before. Capturing their attention and turning it into revenue requires a whole new approach. The Conversion Code provides clear guidance for conquering the new paradigm shift toward online lead generation and inside sales.

Traditional sales and marketing advice is becoming less and less relevant. This book addresses the importance of *purposeful* Internet lead generation and conversion, instead of passive lead generation and conversion. You'll actually learn how to *generate* demand instead of just fulfilling it.

People used to sit through two-minute commercials and couldn't fast-forward them. Now our attention is everywhere...which means it's nowhere for long. In fact, a recent study by Silverpop says you have eight seconds to capture someone's attention online before they move on to the next thing.[1]

HOW YOU CAN CRACK THE CONVERSION CODE

Like any code, The Conversion Code has multiple steps. There is insanely valuable information in each, but I want to give YOU the help YOU need most, right now. I am keenly aware that many salespeople do NOT have to generate their own leads OR even set their own appointments. They simply work for a company (like Quicken Loans or Curaytor) that does that for them. I am also aware that most marketers *never* make sales calls (sad, but true). So think of this as a choose-your-own-adventure book and ask yourself the following questions before you get started.

Do you need to generate more leads now? Is your problem that you just don't have enough people to talk to about what you sell? Start with Section One.

After you read and do what you learn in Section One, you'll have a consistent flow of quality Internet leads.

I know it might seem impossible to have new leads in your inbox each and every day, but I can tell you from my experience that it's not. In fact it's fairly easy if you know exactly what to do.

Do you already have Internet leads, but need help turning them into sales appointments? Section Two is where you should start. Using specific tools and tactics, I will teach you how to create appointments with Internet leads so that you are pitching to new (and old) prospects every single day.

Do you already have plenty of leads to call right now and you just need to know what to say to close them? You're going to want to start with Section Three, which covers exactly what to say to get leads to buy from you.

Inside each section is an easy-to-follow blueprint for improving your business *right now*. The fundamentals of sales and marketing have changed. Have you? I'm going to share with you what the new pillars of sales and marketing really are.

One of my first sales coaches was a telemarketing genius who taught me more about inside sales than any one person has. He would give a powerful 15- to 20-minute lesson on selling each morning before we started pounding the phones, calling leads. It was actually the only time he ever spoke to us. . . .

I remember he loved to say, "Most of you will *learn* more than you will ever *earn* while you work here." Boy, was he right (even though I also earned a lot while there). There was one sketch in particular that he drew that perfectly conveys what you will learn, and then do day after day, because you read this book. It is a very simple drawing, yet it is branded into my brain, and I recommend that you engrave it into yours as well. I think about it with *every* marketing campaign I craft and on every sales call I make. It's shown in Figure I.1.

He used the graph to explain why enthusiasm and timing matter so much when you are selling over the phone. He said the "iasm" from enthusiasm stood for **I Am Sold Myself** (see Figure I.2).

Your job on the phone when talking to leads is actually very simple: to be so enthusiastic about the product you sell that you get them over that buying line. Then and only then can you close them. The same drawing also applies nicely to marketing. It's just that you have

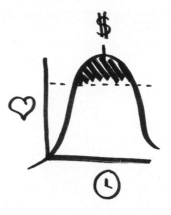

Figure I.1

to get them more excited than the "cost" of them giving you their contact information. Then and only then can you capture them.

Exactly what, when, and how to say things to actually make this happen are all covered in this book and a critical part of my "code."

I was sad to learn after I left Fashion Rock that my sales coach had actually been arrested nine years earlier on federal bank fraud charges for his involvement in a telemarketing operation. He had actually developed a script that was too good, because it crossed several ethical lines and contained bold-faced lies.

Figure I.2

If Lou Pearlman's company was a "black hat" sales organization, Quicken Loans was where I learned "white hat" selling. Quicken Loans taught me more in five weeks of sales training than any university could have in four years.

Another a-ha! moment worth sharing about inside sales (before we get into the X's and O's of lead generation and conversion) came courtesy of Dan Gilbert during my new hire orientation in Michigan. He spoke about Albert Mehrabian's 7-38-55 Percent Rule and the science behind how humans communicate. Gilbert explained that how

HOW HUMANS COMMUNICATE

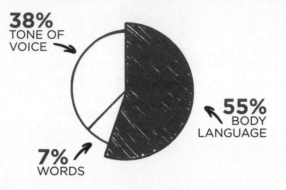

Figure I.3   How Humans Communicate

people communicate actually breaks down into only three buckets (see Figure I.3).

The first and most significant impact on human communication is actually body language. Bad news, he said. When you are selling over the phone to an Internet lead, body language is *gone*.

The next is tone. This is where I shine. I am a wordsmith, but I'm also from the south and I talk slow. I sound super trustworthy over the phone, but also smart. Honest, but sharp. Educated, but not "better than you." It is very difficult to teach people how to improve their tone, but let me make it *very* clear upfront that the words in the script that you will learn in this book work *a lot* better if your tone is great. In fact, if you add tone and body language (everything *but* the actual words you say), it is 93 percent of how humans communicate.

This is why you hear quips like "motion creates emotion" and why you often see inside sales reps standing and selling (or throwing a football to one another) as they talk to a lead. It gets their blood pumping, makes the long days of dialing for dollars a little more bearable, but most importantly, it improves their tone! I sold more vacations in one day than most of the salespeople alongside me sold in a week. I wrote more loans in my first week at Quicken Loans than most of their seasoned bankers wrote in an entire month. I can assure you that my words and looks were not why people were buying. I barely knew what I was talking about ("fake it 'til you make it" comes to mind) and they couldn't see me. My success out of the gate was simply my enthusiastic tone, plus the company providing me with a proven script and solid leads.

Having worked with some extremely talented people during my career, I noticed that the BEST inside salespeople have the following trait: They have a very positive mental attitude. In fact, they have a "black Lab mind-set"—they are happy to see every lead (thanks to Estately CEO Galen Ward for sharing that great analogy with me). The best inside sales reps also work *hard* and put in *effort, daily*. Plus, they are constantly sharpening their axe and looking for *more knowledge* about how they can get even better at sales and closing people.

If you're a business, what do you need to thrive in today's Internet era? The same things that you needed a decade ago and you will still need a decade from now. You need leads, appointments, and sales. In this book, I'll teach you how to get all three.

Because every lead is now an Internet lead, demand for marketing automation and inside sales is *way* up. Inside sales is growing like crazy *because* the Internet is growing like crazy. Being good at traditional marketing and belly-to-belly sales does *not* make you good at Internet marketing and inside sales.

Most of the advice and books about marketing and sales were conceived in the pre-social media, pre-mobile era by people who have *never* had to call even one Internet lead. I'm a fan of legendary sales trainers like Zig Ziglar and Brian Tracy, but they never had to call 10,000+ Internet leads and close them to feed their kids. These are new trends that require a new approach, a new script, and a new coach. Unless you have actually called hundreds of Internet leads a week, for years, you simply can't teach what is in this book.

What you say, *how* you say it, and *when* you say it matter a lot. There has been infinitely more innovation in the marketing world than in the sales world. What you say on a call with an Internet lead is as complex and scientific as the marketing automation campaigns marketers build and launch using HubSpot or Infusionsoft. In Section Three of this book you will learn a new proven script that I crafted specifically for web leads.

THE CONVERSION CODE CREEDS

The Conversion Code is packed with the science of sales and marketing. I'm going to teach you many concepts, formulas, and technical elements that will improve your business. But if you ever feel overwhelmed, I want you to stay focused on the fundamentals. I call them The Conversion Code Creeds, and there is one for each section of the book. Write them down, print them out, and hang them in your cubicle.

The Conversion Code Marketer's Creed

Leads are people too
Image is everything
Facebook is the Internet
Analytics are overrated
Every word counts

The Conversion Code Scheduler's Creed

Every second matters
Zero cold calls
Human companies win
The fortune is in the follow-up
Every word counts

The Conversion Code Closer's Creed

Yes is not an accident
Conversations create clients
Dig deep or go to sleep
You're in charge
Every word counts

The Conversion Code will resharpen your marketing and sales axe for the new, modern Internet-driven era and help you consistently crush your quota. Enjoy!

Part

I

Capture Internet Leads

THE MARKETER'S CREED

LEADS
ARE
PEOPLE TOO

IMAGE IS
EVERYTHING

FACEBOOK
IS **THE**
INTERNET

ANALYTICS
ARE
OVERRATED

EVERY WORD **COUNTS**

#TheConversionCode

Chapter 1

Need More Leads?

How to Build Websites and Landing Pages That Consistently Capture Internet Leads

I f you are reading this book, there is a good chance that you have heard (possibly even a nauseating number of times) that if you want to win online, "content is king."

CONTENT IS NOT KING IF YOUR GOAL IS CAPTURING AND CONVERTING LEADS—DESIGN, BEING PURPOSEFUL AND LANDING PAGES ARE KING

When building your website or landing pages (or changing and improving the ones you may already have), a "conversion-first" approach to design and user experience is a must. Simply put: Great design builds trust and trust is and always has been why people buy things, online and off. As Zig Ziglar once said, "If people like you, they'll listen to you. But if they trust you, they'll do business with you."

In this chapter, I will cover the best ways to capture quality Internet leads using a website and landing pages. In the real world, before you invite anyone over for dinner you clean your house. Online is no different. Before we can send traffic to our website we need to make sure it will convert. Sadly, I see far too many companies that have a website so poorly designed that they are even willing to admit they wouldn't hire themselves based on it.

Because almost every business already has a website, I will start with that. But not before I mention that a critical component of cracking The Conversion Code is to understand that for online lead generation and conversion, landing pages are a much better option than websites.

Ideally, a company will be using both. But if you are reading this and you *really* need leads as quickly as possible, landing pages are the better choice.

How to Build a Website That Builds Trust and Captures Leads

Recent research[1] (which I discovered thanks to Social Triggers founder Derek Halpern, who was a guest on our podcast) conducted by Elizabeth Sillence, Pam Briggs, and Lesley Fishwick, entitled "Trust and Mistrust of Online Health Sites," proves that design online = trust and sales. Here is an excerpt from their study and what they learned:

> *Do different design and information content factors influence trust and mistrust of online health sites? Fifteen women faced with a risky health decision were observed while searching the Internet for information and advice over four consecutive weeks. Women at various stages of menopause participated in the study (41–60+ years, mean age 49). All the women were interested in finding out more about the menopause and all used the Internet at least once a week, although they had different degrees of confidence with respect to being online.*
>
> *Participants discussed their first impressions of a website. There were two factors that led them to reject or mistrust a website quickly. The overwhelming majority of comments related to the design of the website.*

Ninety-four percent cited design and only 6 percent cited content in relation to "the number of times a factor was mentioned as a percentage of the total number of comments about rejection." So maybe content isn't king after all. . . .

Here were some of the women's first impressions and remarks about website design (or lack thereof):

> "I found the screen too busy. I couldn't quite latch onto anything straight away" *(female, 66 years old).*
> "It's so clinical, so pasty, lots of white lots of pale blue obviously trying to be gentle on the eye" *(female, 43 years old).*

"The banners, when they are trying to sell you something or click down here for your free whatever, you just get turned off" *(female, 49 years old)*.

"One of them I didn't like the color of. I couldn't wait to get out. It was an insipid green backdrop it just put me off reading it" *(female, 53 years old)*.

"There was just nothing I liked about it at all. I didn't like the colors, the text, the layout" *(female, 52 years old)*.

This honest, harsh feedback from the participants reminded me of the famous David Ogilvy quote: "The consumer isn't a moron; she is your wife."

If you are going to capture and convert quality Internet leads, you need to gain their trust. Start with their list of critiques and look at your current website to see what you are "guilty" of.

The principles of good web design hold true across demographics. Code Academy, an online interactive program that offers free coding classes (and likely represents a totally different demographic than the aforementioned study), offered eerily similar advice[2] to the women in the health site study.

In September 2015, even the U.S. government crafted design standards for all of its sites moving forward.[3] If middle-aged women, coders, and politicians all agree about the importance of good web design, doesn't it seem foolish to ignore them and not make some changes to your site?

Here's a combination of design principles that showed up on lists from the aforementioned Baby Boomers, Brainiacs, and Bureaucrats. I have also added my interpretation as to why these principles matter so much.

One Column.   Having a one-column layout allows for a "one page, one purpose" approach. Two- and three-column website designs can feel cluttered, complex, and busy. Plus, it's much easier to make a one-column layout responsive for mobile devices, which is where more than 50% of your traffic and leads will come from. If you are going to use a platform like Wordpress or Squarespace to build your website, be sure to look for one-column themes.

Social Proof.   "They are great" is the new "We are great." When you display the feedback of your happiest customers, and not just your own marketing messages, you will find that the quantity and quality of your leads from your website will increase.

Using actual reviews from Yelp, Google, or Facebook and rec-ommendations from LinkedIn is ideal. Remember, your leads can instantly identify and already trust those logos much more so than yours. It amazes me how many business owners have GREAT reviews online, but they don't actually showcase those reviews on their own website in a beautiful way.

In fact, "88% of consumers say they trust online reviews as much as personal recommendations."[4]

More Contrast. The fewer colors you use, the more the colors you do use will "pop." Whitespace is highly underrated. A well-designed website should get people to the parts of it that make you money, fast. Increase your contrast by taking a "less is more" approach: Use col-ors only when critical—like in your calls to action. This will get the people visiting your site clicking on the pages, buttons, and links you want them to the most.

Fewer Form Fields. We have only eight seconds to capture some-one's attention online, so you cannot ask for a ton of information on your website contact forms. Stick to the basics of name, phone num-ber, and email when possible. You can also use a "log in with Facebook or Google" button above or below the form fields so they can complete the form without any keystrokes at all.

I have also found it to be VERY helpful to have a backup option like "Or you can call/text 555-5555 or email Hello@Curaytor.com" any-time you have a contact form. The bottom line is that if someone is willing to fill out a form on your website to be contacted they might also prefer to simply contact you right then. If it takes someone more than a moment or two to locate your phone number and your email address on your website, fix that ASAP.

Keeping Focus. More choices = fewer decisions made. You really want to limit the number of calls to action on any given page to one, when you can. If one page of your website asks me to join your newsletter, follow you on Twitter, *and* download your e-book, I probably won't do any of them. Remember, one page = one purpose. The only page of your site that will likely need multiple CTAs (calls to action) is your homepage. For all other pages, keep them laser focused on one primary goal.

Larger Targets. This one is particularly important to lead capture. Code Academy cited Fitt's Law, which says, "the time required to move and interact with a target area is a function of the distance and size of the target. The closer and larger the target, the faster the action." To state it simply: the size of and distance between the form fields on your website forms and landing pages matter. Make sure your forms are not too small and also not too spaced out.

Design for Edge Cases.   Many of your website's visitors will be coming back to visit for a second, third, or even hundredth time. But some of your website visitors will be visiting for the first time, especially after I help you crack the Facebook ads code and start sending new leads there each and every day. It is also safe to say that many online consumers do not want to call a company they find on the Internet. But for the "edge cases" who do, shouldn't your phone number be easy to find? The bottom line is that even the best-built websites do not capture every visitor who stops by. Just make sure it captures every serious buyer who visits. And make sure the visitors who are the "edge case" (don't visit often and are unfamiliar with you and your brand) feel as welcome as the visitors who return often.

If you are planning on building a new website, let the information found in those consumer insights and design principles be your guide. That doesn't go just for those of you who are trying to DIY (do it yourself)—believe me, I've been there. Platforms like WordPress and Squarespace make building beautiful websites, and then adding extras, a snap and inexpensive. But there is a real cost to trying to design and build websites yourself. Even when you download a "theme" that looks great, there will still be a lot of work to do to set it up properly.

Years ago, I spent hours and hours obsessing and working on a website called Tech Savvy Agent that I started and ran with my good friend Steve Pacinelli. We spent *hours* and many sleepless nights designing, building, and customizing it.

It was *terrible*. Our idea of being creative was going completely against common sense and web standards, like using a black background with teal text. Thank God our content was great and the web design bar was still so low then or no one would have put up with the gaudiness.

When we finally went with a professional web designer, things exploded. We reinvested what we got out of our first DIY site and hired a developer/designer (Ken Granger) to create a custom WordPress site for us for $5,000. We launched our first professionally designed site in May 2010. Up to that point, we'd never achieved more than 1,000 page views in one day. All of a sudden, we had navigation aids, bright/contrasting colors, and so forth. The results were instant and dramatic.

The first day with our new site, we had three times as many page views as we had ever gotten in a single day! Better yet, because we continued to crank out great content, we were able to maintain that traffic day over day for quite a while. As soon as I saw that 3,000 page views in a day was possible, I immediately set my sights on a bigger goal: 100,000 page views in one month. I knew we had a real shot at it, and I believed we could do it in the first 12 months with the new, professionally designed site.

Imagine my surprise when we achieved that goal in the first 30 days that we tried to. Once we surrounded our great content with great design, we were on track for over a million page views a year! The ugly duckling had officially become a swan. Don't underestimate the value of hiring a professional who does great design when building your website and landing pages.

If you're updating your website out of the dark ages, do yourself a favor: Hire a professional. Have them build you a website that doesn't just look good for this year, but be willing to pay to keep it updated for years to come. Design standards change, fast. Give the list of design principles in this chapter to your designer (or use them yourself if you insist on the DIY approach) and make sure your new site adheres to them. The upside of doing so can be swift and drastic.

HOW TO QUICKLY AND INEXPENSIVELY TURN A WEBSITE INTO A LEAD-GENERATING MACHINE

Building a well-designed new website can be a daunting, lengthy, and expensive task. The good news is there are some hacks for turning (almost) any website into a lead-generating machine, instantly. Remember, we do not want to start sending traffic to our website until we have a well-oiled mousetrap with fresh cheese set.

There are some proven tactics and website add-ons that will start to increase the overall percentage of your visits-to-leads captured (often called the conversion rate). Everyone seems to have their own personal preference for the amount of proactive calls to action on a site. As the ladies in the research pointed out, you do not want to overwhelm people. As the 49-year-old woman noted, *"The banners, when they are trying to sell you something or click down here for your free whatever, you just get turned off."*

It's not that banners or pop-ups or "house ads" don't work and should not be a part of your website. In fact, they are critical pieces of cracking The Conversion Code. But if you do have to annoy or trick a lead to capture their information, you will have a much harder time converting them into a conversation by email or into becoming a customer over the phone. First impressions matter.

Our goal is to be there for those who want to buy now or speak with someone in sales, but while ALSO capturing the information of and keeping track of those who will buy later.

Here are some proven ways to capture leads on your website, without being (too) annoying. Be sure to also apply solid design principles to these elements when adding them to your site:

- "Alert" box (Intercom, Kissmetrics Engage, and HelloBar all offer this)
- Live Chat (Intercom, Zopim, and Olark are all great choices)
- Full-screen pop-up (that is well timed using exit intent or the visitors behavior) (Intercom, Kissmetrics Engage, OptinMonster)
- Contact information in the header or footer (be sure the phone number, email address, and physical address are clearly visible and clickable)
- A dedicated Contact page that you link to from your About page and Testimonials page and from the website navigation menu/header/footer. This page can have a form, but should also have any other way possible to contact you (like social media channels)
- An alternate "Call, Text, Live Chat or Email Us Instead" option on every contact form

SumoMe is a great option if you want to plug and play most of these features into your existing website, all at once. I especially like SumoMe's Welcome Mat, List Builder, and Scroll Box add ons. Thankfully, SumoMe, Kissmetrics, and Intercom all make adding these features as simple as installing a line or two of code into your site.

One of the best features of real-time, live chat in the modern era that few companies are taking advantage of is contextual messages and triggers. If someone visits a specific page of your site, or if they visit a certain number of pages or spend enough total time on your site, these tools can trigger a message that is uber-specific. As an example, if someone is on the Testimonials page of your website, the live chat pop-up or alert badge can read, "Thanks for reading our reviews, Chris. I always read reviews before I buy things too. If you have any questions let me know!" or if someone read several articles on your blog, a dynamic message could trigger and say, "High five! You just read four awesome articles, in a row. You may want to subscribe to our email newsletter for new blog posts." The possibilities are really endless. To keep it simple, just think about (a) What triggers do you want to use? and (b) What messages/links/paths do you want to display when those triggers are activated by a visitor?

These behavior-based website "messages" (which can also be extended to email marketing messages covered on page 66) personalize the experience for the visitor and give them every opportunity to connect in a relevant, semi-automated-for-you way, without being too creepy or annoying.

For a more traditional "live chat," Olark and Zopim both make great tools that can easily be integrated into nearly any existing website in just a few minutes. Think of your website like a retail store. If you follow The Conversion Code, thousands of people are going to walk in each month. By having someone available in case they are not "just browsing," you truly provide an appreciated service to the serious buyers who want more help, but may not quite be ready to fill out a form or call you.

The key to all of these real-time messaging tools is to *be available*. You may not be able to be on 24/7, but remember: Just like it is critical to call an Internet lead immediately, the same is true for live chat. The nice thing is that once you have this installed on your site, you will get a push alert each time someone engages with the automated, customized chat tool. Make sure that on each and every

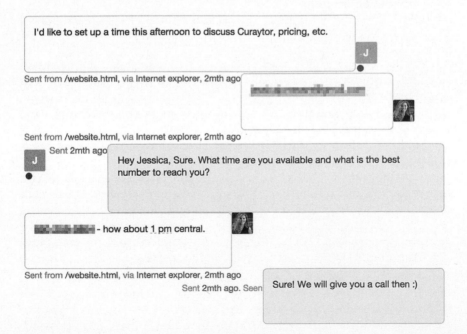

Figure 1.1

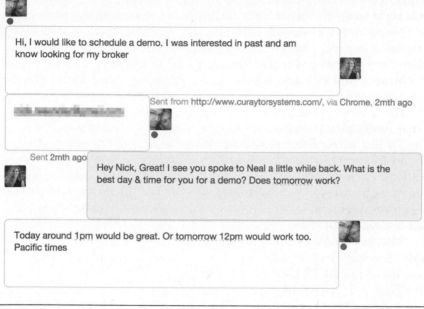

Figure 1.2

chat your purpose is to be helpful, but also to *get their information* (name, email, phone number). They will want to use the chat to get a quick response; you want to use the chat to book an appointment or get them on the phone as quickly as possible.

Here is an example of an actual live chat that led to a conversion. Be sure to pay close attention to how our team doesn't benefit dump about what we do when we have a hot, live chat lead. Instead, they focus on booking them for an appointment with sales and getting their phone number (see Figure 1.1).

Figure 1.2 shows another example of just how hot live chat leads can be.

I have found that live chat leads are some of the *best* leads. If you have not been getting them until now, enjoy. If you have had live chat installed, but were not using it the right way, you will find that using these best practices will consistently get you quality appointments for your sales team. You want a lead on your calendar, not on your website! Live chat makes that transition from marketing to sales seamless.

LANDING PAGES ARE THE NEW BLACK

In 2003, the IT department at Microsoft invented landing pages in response to poor online sales of their flagship business product, Office.

The reason landing pages are so effective for online lead generation is simple: They have only ONE purpose. Compare that to your website or blog, which may have dozens of navigation options or categories to choose from, and you can see why professional marketers use landing pages when money is on the line and ROI is a must.

Here is how Wikipedia defines a landing page (and why we should all thank Microsoft's IT guys for inventing them):

> *A landing page, sometimes known as a "lead capture page," is a single web page that appears in response to clicking on a search engine–optimized search result or an online advertisement. The landing page will usually display directed sales copy that is a logical extension of the advertisement, search result or link. Landing pages are often linked to from social media, email campaigns or search engine marketing campaigns in order to enhance the effectiveness of the advertisements.*

> *The general goal of a landing page is to convert site visitors into sales or leads.*

> *If the goal is to obtain a lead, the landing page will include some method for the visitor to get into contact, usually a phone number, or an inquiry form.*

Here is the part of that blurb *The Conversion Code* laser focuses on and what can get you leads and appointments today: "Landing pages are often linked to from social media, email campaigns."

Unlike website traffic that Google can bring you through SEO and SEM, where the "preview" of the ad or link is very text-based, social media and email marketing allow you to be very visual and descriptive about what you sell BEFORE the user clicks, which can drastically increase the conversion rate of the landing page you send them to.

I will go much deeper on Facebook ad and email marketing landing page strategies on pages 48 and 18.

But before you start sending people to your landing pages, just like we did with your website's design and user experience, we need to clean up the landing pages you may already have. More likely, you need to start over and build new, optimized landing pages that capture the names, phone numbers, and email addresses of leads day in and day out. Here's how.

There are many proven best practices regarding landing page design that I will cover ahead. Keep in mind that even if you have no design or technical skill whatsoever, there are some very cool companies like LeadPages, Instapage, or Unbounce that let you build inexpensive (or free) landing pages in just a few easy clicks. Be sure to search their existing themes by keyword like "real estate" to find pre-built, industry-centric designs.

Even SumoMe (which I mentioned earlier as a suite of great website plug-ins) built something called WelcomeMat, which is basically a landing page that sits on top of a blog post or the page of your website someone is on (pushing the content "below the fold"). This technology turns virtually every page of a website into a landing page, instantly. Bottom line? All the bells and whistles in the world on a website won't convert better than a singular focused, well-designed landing page will.

MICROWAVE MARKETING MENTALITY

People used to sit through two-minute commercials, and believe it or not, couldn't fast-forward them. They listened to the radio and if an ad came on, they could only change the station to another one with more ads. Today thanks to our phones, watches, and social media addiction, our attention is everywhere, which means it's nowhere for very long. In fact, recent studies say you have eight seconds to capture someone's attention before they move on to the next thing. That's four less seconds than in the year 2,000 and one second less than a goldfish's attention span!

Because our brains process visuals 60,000 times faster than they do text, a critical component of cracking The Conversion Code is to understand that design, not words, builds trust online. Words matter, sure. In fact, copywriting should be an obsession for every business that wants to be successful using the Internet. Writing great WEB copy for Facebook ads, lead follow-up emails, Tweets, and so forth is a new skill set most are missing. But if you want an online consumer to actually read what you write, you actually need an "image is everything" mind-set.

From the takeaway-laden Silverpop report I referenced in "How to Crack The Conversion Code," which addresses this attention-span dilemma, I learned that "Members of Silverpop's Strategic Research Team first registered to receive emails from 150 companies throughout North America and the United Kingdom—40 B2B companies and 110 B2C." The team evaluated the quality and performance of the landing pages reached after users clicked on the main call to action in emails. This technique of getting existing leads to re-opt in, and thus prove they are still very engaged, through a new landing page sent by mass email is one every company should be using.

In the study, they evaluated for things like readable URLs, repetition in email and landing page copy, primary conversion goals, consistency and quality of design, placement of primary CTA, inclusion of navigation bars, use of forms, length of copy, use of subheadings, types and number of links, opt-in requests, and more. Here are the six key findings from the report:

1. "Successful landing pages grab attention quickly by matching the promotional copy in the email's call-to-action that yielded the click. Yet 45 percent of the landing pages evaluated failed to repeat the email's promotional copy in the headline."
2. "Catapulting a clicker to a Web site's home page generally fails to deliver on the promise inherent in the email's call-to-action. Yet 17 percent of email campaigns dumped recipients there."
3. "Recipients can be taken aback when they click on a link and end up on a landing page without the same look and feel as the email that captured their attention. But three out of 10 marketers risked confusing customers and prospects by sending them to landing pages not matching the email."
4. "Asking too many questions can lead prospective customers to become wary and frustrated enough that they abandon the process. Nevertheless, 45 percent of landing pages that included forms required more than 10 fields to be completed."
5. "While the presence of a navigation bar on a landing page can be a distraction that pulls visitors away from the primary conversion goal, nearly seven out of 10 landing pages included them."
6. "Professional writers know it's a lot harder to write short copy than long. Apparently some marketers are taking the easy way out, since 25 percent of the landing pages reviewed by Silverpop required scrolling through more than two screens of text."

Another great resource for landing page optimization advice came from the Kissmetrics blog in their post entitled "Anatomy of a Perfect Landing Page." And while they do start the post by admitting, "Although there is no exact formula to making a perfect landing page," the way they visualized and numbered the elements of a "perfect" page were spot on.

Here are the nine key elements Kissmetrics identified that make a perfect landing page (with my take on each):

1. **Headline:** Make it clear, concise, and "coupled." The headline of your landing page needs to be an extension of the ad, email, or link that brought them to it. If what brought them to the

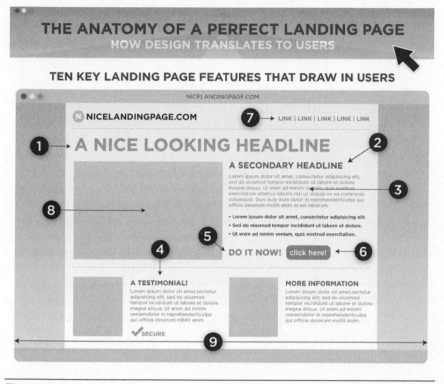

THE ANATOMY OF A PERFECT LANDING PAGE
HOW DESIGN TRANSLATES TO USERS

TEN KEY LANDING PAGE FEATURES THAT DRAW IN USERS

Figure 1.3

page was an offer to "Get Your Home's Value" or "Free eBook about Facebook Ads," you would basically want to repeat that as closely as you can with your headline. Remember, you have eight seconds (four seconds less than you had a decade ago) tops to keep their attention. Don't get too cute with the copy of the headline, or the rest of this list won't matter.

2. **Subheadline**: With the subheadline, we simply want to continue them down the path the headline started them on. If "Get Your Home's Value" or "Free eBook about Facebook Ads" were the headline, a good subheadline would be "Home Value Report Will Be 100% Accurate as of Today's Date" or "27 Facebook Ads You Can Run Today for More Leads."

3. **Description**: Make sure you triple-check all grammar, punctuation, and spelling (Grammarly can help with this if you know you screw up often). This holds true of ALL copy I will cover in this book. Landing page descriptions, Facebook ads (page 48), blog posts (page 21), emails and SMS messages (page 91) should all be looked at with a microscope before

being published and promoted. If you want someone to buy from you, or at least pick up the phone when you call, words matter. All of them. Just like when you sell over the phone you do not have the luxury of visual cues, online you might have *only* words. So use a scalpel with your copy, not an axe.

4. **Testimonial**: The goal here is to establish trust quickly. Using positive reviews (and a nice visual icon near the written testimonial) from well-known and trusted websites like Yelp, Facebook, or LinkedIn can really have an impact. This is not a new practice, but many companies are still touting their BBB (Better Business Bureau) credentials over their consumer-facing reviews. But even those old-school "verified by" or "trusted by" visual cues increase conversions. When eyeglass company AC Lens started using VeriSign, it saw a 41 percent increase in conversions. Always remember, trust is why we have always bought and why we will always buy things. Building digital trust is still building trust.

5. **Call to action**: When the visitor is ready, your call to action must be obvious, easy to find, the right color, and contain the right copy. Avoid words like "Register" or "Subscribe," and instead try things like "View Now," "Download," "Unlock," or "Get Instant Access." Mozilla, the makers of the popular Firefox browser, increased their conversions by 3.6 percent by simply changing the button copy from "Try Firefox 3" to "Download Now—Free."[5] The landing page tools I mentioned earlier, like LeadPages and Unbounce, also make A/B testing landing pages, buttons, colors, and copy very easy to do. Don't be afraid to try, test, and change your calls to action often, but once you find the ones that work best, run with them.

6. **Clickable button(s)**: A conversion button should stand out and be near/below the call to action, either accompanying the message or reiterating it word for word. Kissmetrics advises, "the button should be big, bright, and above where a user would have to scroll to it. Orange or yellow buttons for a CTA help to catch a viewer's eye." Again, there are no universal rules (meaning green buttons or red buttons can also work well), but this is a great foundation to follow.

7. **Remove links**: Landing pages have one purpose, so there really shouldn't be many (if any) links to other things. This will take the visitor away, defeating the purpose of getting them there to capture their information in the first place. Sometimes you do have to link back to your main website or even a Terms of

Service/Privacy Policy page to be in line with ad guidelines, but be extremely cautious about having links on your landing pages. Remember, this isn't your website. You do not need normal navigation options. You need leads!

8. **Image or video**: I am a fan of a "hero shot" versus a collage of pictures. Also, there is no need for more text on top of the image or video. This can clutter the design. Try thinking of your images or videos for your landing pages in this context, best described by my friend Matthew Shadbolt from the *New York Times*: If someone were scrolling through their Facebook newsfeed and saw your image, would it have stopping power? I'll further discuss the importance of images in Facebook ads (page 51) and blog posts (page 23), but they are just as important as an element for your landing pages (and website). If you need great stock photos that aren't supercheesy, try visiting the royalty-free, for-business-use sections of StockUp, Pexels, and ShutterStock.

9. **Stay above the fold**: Considering that many of the people visiting your landing pages will be on a mobile device (you have only eight seconds to keep their attention regardless of what device they are on) you really need to maximize what appears above the fold on your landing page. "Above the fold" just means what they can see and interact with, without scrolling down. There is a time and place for long-form landing pages that have a ton of sales copy (even multipage landing pages), but for the most part an "above the fold" mind-set is the one to have.

One of my favorite parts of LeadPages is that you can actually sort all of their landing pages by Conversion Rate. You are able to practically apply lessons that others learned without having to build an ineffective landing page yourself first. Take one of their highest-performing templates from your industry and quickly edit it to make it your own. This does not ensure that you will have success, but training wheels and "big data" can be truly helpful here. You will find that many of their top performers follow most, if not all, of these nine key elements.

If you want to spend a few hours learning more about how small changes in website design, landing pages, calls to action, buttons, images, and copywriting can impact lead conversion rates, I highly recommend that you check out WhichTestWon.com. They have hundreds of A/B tests you can learn from. You even get to, as the name implies, guess which variant won. You will be surprised at how often which test you think won actually lost!

GET THE MOST OUT OF YOUR WEBSITE AND LANDING PAGES BY RETARGETING THE VISITORS WHO DO NOT CONVERT

Even the best websites and landing pages with all the well-placed widgets in the world will not convert every visitor into a lead. Thankfully, you can "retarget" those who visit and do not convert. When I interviewed AdStage CEO Sahil Jain, he called it "tagging the shark." You can't get every shark on your hook and into a boat to observe, but you can at least tag most of them to observe over time. Retargeting online is very similar. Every visitor who does not become a lead can begin to immediately see your ads on Facebook, across the web, and in mobile apps. This can really turn your website into a relationship in a world where most websites have a one-night stand with their visitors. If they don't close them on the first try, they never call back. HUGE mistake.

In later chapters, we will discuss a plethora of strategies and tactics that will get free and paid traffic to your site. Many of the tips you already learned can get you a very high conversion rate, but it will almost never be higher than the rate of visitors who do not convert. Many of the landing pages you will build and use will capture less than 90 percent of the people who visit them. A Marketing Sherpa reader study revealed landing page conversion averages were between 5 and 11 percent when linking to a landing page for a free or paid offer via an email.[6] The conversion rate from Facebook and Google ads can be even lower. This is why following those who do not convert with more chances is a must. They showed intent by visiting your "store"—they just didn't complete a form or contact you. Retargeting allows you to move your ads in front of them in real time as they continue to "shop" online. If you have ever been on Amazon looking at a product only to see it in an ad in your Facebook Newsfeed shortly thereafter you have experienced retargeting.

You can also use a more advanced, pro tool like Driftrock so that your entire database and email list is also being "retargeted" in nearly real time. Imagine a real estate agent getting a lead from Zillow that automatically went into their CRM and then that lead seeing an ad for the real estate agent, or a comparable home, the next time they logged into Facebook or visited CNN.com.

Retargeting works by tracking cookies, pixels, phone numbers, or emails. We currently use the native Facebook tracking pixel for newsfeed, web, and mobile retargeting ads, and we have also used AdRoll for retargeting across the web. In Section Two, I go deeper on using retargeting as a lead follow-up and appointment-setting tool.

Now you know why I advised that you *purposefully* start The Conversion Code by cleaning up your online "home" (website and landing pages) before you invite over "company" (traffic and leads). With a website design that converts, landing pages that capture, and retargeting firing on all cylinders, I will now teach you how to write a perfect blog post that is optimized for search engines, social media, and lead generation.

Chapter 2

Writing the Perfect Blog Post

Before I dive into the X's and O's of optimizing your content for distribution in Chapter 3, I want to start with the importance of optimizing the structure of the content. When you are creating content online, formatting is critical. In Chapter 1, I covered how to format your websites and landing pages for maximum lead generation. Now we need to populate your site with content. The easiest way to do that is by using a blog.

Let me be clear before I get into the blogging tips. I am a fan of business, not blogging. But I can tell you from my personal journey and experiences that statistics like, "Marketers who have prioritized blogging are 13x more likely to enjoy positive ROI."[1] and "79% of companies that have a blog report a positive ROI for inbound marketing"[2] hold true.

The more content I have created, the more cash I have collected. Period. And even across our customer base at Curaytor, the "ROI" and happiness of our clients, who pay us tens of thousands of dollars for our help, often comes down to their willingness and capacity to execute our blogging strategy.

If you 100% know you will NOT blog, consider doing what we coach our Curaytor clients to do. Hire someone else to do it! We hired a professional journalist (Paul Hagey) at Curaytor and the ROI has been tremendous. Often, bloggers, journalists, and writers are greatly undervalued and underpaid. So we overvalue them and overpay them. The results speak for themselves. If you don't know anyone locally, try using Upwork or Freelancer to find help with quality content creation. Even if you don't have a large budget, these websites thrive by offering you the ability to hire people on a one off, not full-time, basis.

Whether you take the lead on blogging or you decide to outsource it, you want to get the most out of each and every post you publish. So, let's take a look at what a "perfect" blog post looks like.

Buffer, a social media scheduling tool used by millions, recently identified several essential elements of a post in an article called "The Anatomy of a Perfect Blog Post."[3] Here are the ones that I felt mattered the most from Buffer's great list.

HEADLINE

These are the words that count the most. Buffer and Copyblogger (two great resources that I highly recommend) identified that approximately 8 out of 10 people will read a headline, but only 2 out of 10 people will read the rest. Your ability to "convert" them into diving deeper will be directly proportionate to your ability to write great headlines. I often spend longer on a headline than I do on a post. I am constantly thinking of headlines and adding them into draft mode on my blog to work more on later. When I get stuck on a headline, I write the entire article and edit it, and usually by the end of that process I know the headline that makes the most sense.

Buffer also gave some great headline strategies that are "backed by psychology." Read these examples and tell me if you recognize any of these styles from some of the buzziest sites going today:

Surprise: "This Is Not a Perfect Blog Post (But It Could've Been)"
Questions: "Do You Know How to Create the Perfect Blog Post?"
Curiosity gap: "Ten Ingredients in a Perfect Blog Post. Number 9 Is Impossible!"
Negatives: "Never Write a Boring Blog Post Again"
How to: "How to Create a Perfect Blog Post"
Numbers: "Ten Tips to Creating a Perfect Blog Post"
Audience referencing: "For People on the Verge of Writing the Perfect Blog Post"
Specificity: "The Six-Part Process to Getting Twice the Traffic to Your Blog Post"

STORYTELLING HOOK

Once the headline is nailed, storytelling is a must. In fact, when Alex Turnbull and the Groove HQ team tested introductions for their posts, they found that storytelling led to 296 *percent* more full-page readers and a 521 *percent* increase in average time on page than a post without storytelling.[4] What do they mean by storytelling?

Instead of starting a post with "Here are the best iPad apps for real estate agents," the storytelling version would start a little more like this: "After a busy week of working with clients on her clunky PC, real estate agent Susie Smith went to the Apple store last weekend. She had noticed that more and more of her customers were using iPads to look at homes for sale, and she didn't want to fall behind them. Her current laptop was on the verge of laughable. Susie called me when she got back to her office because she wanted to make sure she loaded up her new toy with the best iPad apps for real estate agents. Here are the apps I recommended that Susie download right away. I thought you might like the list as well."

The difference in a blog post with, or without, storytelling is obvious and impactful.

FEWER CHARACTERS PER LINE AT FIRST

When an online visitor clicks through to read your blog post, a huge block of text as the first impression can be overwhelming. Try spacing out the introduction. Using the foregoing example, here is how I would have formatted it to ease the reader in with fewer characters per line at first:

"After a busy week of working with clients on her clunky PC, real estate agent Susie Smith went to the Apple store last weekend.

She had noticed that more and more of her customers were using iPads to look at homes for sale, and she didn't want to fall behind them.

Her current laptop was on the verge of laughable ... Susie called me when she got back to her office because she wanted to make sure she loaded up her new toy with the best iPad apps for real estate agents.

Here are the iPad apps I recommended that Susie download right away. I thought you might like the list as well."

Compare that with text all in one bulky block. It's a big difference! You can see how the spaced-out version does not feel so overwhelming.

I would also extend this fewer characters at first formatting ideology to your email marketing messages (more on page 91).

FEATURED IMAGE

Having at least one awesome image in your blog post is a must. Consider this recent data about the impact of images on press releases from the PRWEB Blog: "Releases with no images had an average time-on-page of 2:18. However, releases that contained images had an average time-on-page of 2:47."[5] That's a 21 percent increase in time spent per page by adding a photo. No brainer.

Adding an image to each individual piece of content clearly helps, but let's also see what happens when you expand this image-first approach to your entire website.

BuildZoom (a marketplace for locating contractors) saw even better results when they added an image to every page on their site. They also shared their results in the foregoing article, finding "the overall time-on-site suddenly increased by about 150 percent, from an average of 1 minute to 2.5 minutes per visitor."[6]

These are HUGE jumps in time on page and time on site, giving you a greater chance to engage or capture a lead, achieved by simply adding great pictures to your content.

Pro tip: There are plenty of free-to-use stock photos out there where you can find great images for your blog posts. At Curaytor, we use *StockUp* and Pexels.

THE 1,500+ WORD SWEET SPOT

SerpIQ and Medium both released some fascinating and helpful data regarding how long a blog post should be. What they discovered was that longer-form content does better in search engines *and* social media.

The average piece of content that reaches page one of Google has more than 2,000 words! You can also see how the ranking of 1–10 was also nearly directly proportionate to the length of the content.

AVG LENGTH OF TOP PERFORMING CONTENT

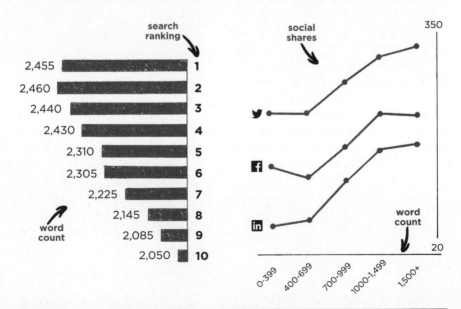

Figure 2.1   Average Length of Top-Performing Content

With social media sharing, one might think a blog post should be short and sweet in order to get shares. Wrong. Look how the word count increasing actually correlates with increased shares on Facebook, Twitter, and LinkedIn.

Medium, a popular blogging platform started by the cofounder of Twitter Ev Williams, also found the "sweet spot" with their readers to be about seven minutes (which equates to approximately 1,600 words).[7]

SOUNDBITES FOR SOCIAL SHARING

After you finish your post, what are the one or two quips or "soundbites" from the post that would be the most socially shareable? Be sure to make these stand out in the post itself. Often, bloggers wait until the end of an article to position their social share calls to action. By highlighting the best parts of your post higher up, you will see an instant increase in virality. ClickToTweet.com (or CoSchedule.com if you are using WordPress) makes adding these soundbites and social calls to action simple.

NOW YOU'RE CREATING CONTENT THAT IS *READY* TO BE OPTIMIZED FOR LEAD GENERATION, SOCIAL MEDIA, AND SEARCH ENGINES

Bonus: Need some inspiration for blog posts?

Now that you understand how to create the perfect blog post, and once you see how "doing it right" can really have an impact, you will probably want to start blogging more. The next time you tell yourself that you do not have time to blog, just remember what you really are not taking time for is lead generation and conversion. In a perfect world you could simply build a website and some landing pages and never have to update them. But in the real world the websites that get the MOST traffic and leads are the ones that emphasize blogging. Plus, by always having new content on your blog you also always have new ammo for your Facebook ads and email marketing campaigns.

Writing online and offline are not that different. You will still get writer's block/fatigue. So with that in mind, here is a curated list of handy ideas for blog posts that can be applied to any industry (you can see the full list of 50 at OptinMonster[8]):

What are some of the common questions that people ask when they email you?

What is your favorite piece of industry news that you've come across recently?

Is there something that has frustrated you recently? Talk about it.
Create a list of the top 10 things you wish you knew when you started.
Give speech notes from a recent presentation you gave.
Have you figured out a way to save a few hours a week?
What would you recommend your customers do in the first few weeks?
Is there an industry leader or influencer you can interview?
Have you used any new tools or applications recently that have helped improve your workflow?
Have you created an ultimate resource post?
What are you particularly passionate about within your industry?
What type of things do you review to determine quality in your industry?
How have you changed how you work over the years?
What is a creative use of your product?
Make a Myth versus Fact post

Now that your website and landing pages are optimized and your blog posts are perfected, let's make sure you're also optimizing your content for lead generation, social media, and search engines.

Optimizing Your Content for Lead Generation, Social Media, and Search Engines

As you learned in Chapter 1, design matters a lot when generating online leads.

In Chapter 2, you learned how to construct the "perfect blog post."

Now you have a website, you have landing pages, and you have some great content.

Optimizing that content for lead generation, social media, and search engines is also important to cracking The Conversion Code, as well as an oft overlooked step by even the savviest and most experienced digital marketers.

Remember, we want the guests at our dinner parties to have the *best experience possible*. Not just enjoy themselves.

There are very specific things that you can do to make your blog posts and social media content go as "viral" as possible. When I use the term "viral," I am not referring to a grumpy cat or Charlie Bit My Finger YouTube video. Viral optimization is the art of architecting your content so it goes as far as it possibly can and generates as many leads as possible.

OPTIMIZING YOUR CONTENT FOR LEAD GENERATION

Let's focus on the most important piece first. Because even if you "get found" in Google, install all the right lead capture plug-ins, and perfectly craft your content for social sharing, it still does not ensure that you will capture as many leads as possible. It is necessary to first optimize your content for lead generation by adding "lead magnets."

What is a lead magnet? Basically, it is something so valuable that someone would give up their name, phone number, and email address to access it. You do not want to make people register to access your website in general, but you do want to force them to register to access certain parts of it or "extras." Most of your lead magnets will live on a landing page featuring an opt-in form that's required for "instant access to X." You want to be sure that when someone completes the request, they get what they asked for immediately and you get their information immediately.

If you have been wondering how you can turn a blog into a business driver, lead magnets are part of the answer. With an assist from Digital Marketer,[1] here are nine examples of lead magnets (and my thoughts on each) that can be applied to any landing page for any business model:

1. **Guide/report/e-book**: When you build a guide, report, or e-book, there is much more perceived value than there is in a blog post. Taking the time to build the "Ultimate Guide to Facebook Ads" or a "Free e-book about Social Media Lead Generation" can really increase your conversions and grow your email list compared to a blog post of a similar style. The e-book doesn't even need to be on Amazon or iBooks. You can simply web host it as a PDF and deliver it that way by email, SMS, or a URL redirect after they register.

2. **Cheat sheet/handout/checklist**: There is SO much content online that downloading a simple "cheat sheet" can actually be an attractive angle. You can find success by offering something like a "Social Media Ideal Image Sizes Cheat Sheet" or an "A–Z Facebook Ads Checklist to Capturing Leads Today." What are the "cheat sheets" consumers you target would find value in? Our real estate clients have found a "Complete List of Open Houses Happening This Weekend" captures thousands of new emails for them!

3. **Toolkit/resource list**: If you were buying a home, you would probably end up using multiple sites, like Zillow, Trulia, Realtor .com, and Homes.com. But there are hundreds of other great sites that consumers are not as aware of. Thus, "37 Amazing Websites You Can Use to Find Your Next Home" would be an example of a great resource list to offer.

4. **Video/webinar training**: For me, video has been king for conversions. Video has given our leads the chance to really get to know me, what we sell, and our company culture even before

our sales team ever calls them. Not everyone is great on video, but there is much more perceived value in a video or webinar than there is in written content. Video has become so important that I recommend finding ways to implement it even if you're not great on camera. Try using screen recordings with ScreenFlow or Camtasia. You can even make and edit your own videos, using simple mobile apps like Animoto, Replay Video Editor, or iMovie. As an example, a post titled "Instantly Watch: Facebook Ads Master Course" or "RSVP: Facebook Ads Webinar" will help you not only capture more leads but also tap into a new kind of lead that prefers video to text.

5. **Software/free trial:** When I worked for DotLoop we used the common freemium model as a lead magnet. You can use our basic (but awesome) software for "free" (in exchange for your information). Then our sales team can call to "upsell" you on the additional features the free version does not include. You can also give away the full version of what you do, but limit the amount of time people can access that trial. Evernote and Dropbox are popular companies that use a free trial as a lead magnet (it must work—I have the paid versions of both).

6. **Discount:** "Want to save money? Create an account now and get a 20 percent discount!" You've probably seen this one, a lot. That is because it works. People love deals. Another technique you'll sometimes see on e-commerce sites is that you can "see the price in the cart." As blindingly obvious a lead magnet and call to action as a sale or promo code is, I am amazed at how many companies don't throw this fastball down the middle often enough.

7. **Quiz/survey:** Maybe you have seen something in your newsfeed like "Are you an 80s baby?" or "Find out what celebrity you would marry!" This "quizification" of content is smart and appealing because there is an immediate payoff (you get to see what you scored and can share it with your friends). You can actually use a site like TryInteract.com or PlayBuzz.com, which makes it very easy to build your own custom quizzes.

8. **Assessment/test:** What I love about "tests" is that you can reach an audience that will *not* contact you, but might at least be willing to see if they should. "Take this test to see if we can help you" vs. "WE DON'T KNOW YOU BUT WE CAN HELP YOU!" Big difference. At Curaytor, we spent time developing a nine-step self-audit for prospective clients to fill out, evaluate their own work, and give us an idea of whether we'd be a good match. People are fascinated with being able to compare their scores to their peers. Tony Robbins uses a disc profile to

assess prospective hires and also gives them out online. He has likely gotten hundreds of thousands of email subscribers by doing this.

9. **Additional sales information**: If the price of what you sell is not on your website, it can become one of the most powerful reasons to "learn more" or "get pricing." Create some mystery and require they provide their information before seeing pricing or availability. This can work especially well if you offer them a "video walkthrough", with pricing at the end. We have generated thousands of leads and sales by offering an eight-minute demo video as a lead magnet.

Do *not* overthink what your lead magnets should or could be.

In real estate, the best lead magnets are listings and home value reports. These are the same things that have *always* been lead magnets for real estate. It's just that pre-Internet they were dangled as a carrot in print.

If you sell loans, the best lead magnet might be accessing today's interest rates or calculating your new lower payment. In the past, leads had to call in to get this information. Moving forward, they may download an app or complete a form online to get it. Either way, a conversion has occurred.

Once you have these lead magnets established for your business, there are two last steps to making sure they get used as often as possible.

First, you have to bake your lead magnets into your website's design. Your menu, header, footer, and pop-up messages can all include links to these magnets/landing pages. Second, you should make sure that *all* of your blog posts have lead magnets inside of them. I actually find that simply adding one or two lead magnets (don't go overboard) into the text of what I write is a great strategy and gets leads coming in consistently.

As an example, if I published a blog post titled "3 Quick Facebook Tips You Can Use Today," I would include a lead magnet like "You can also download our entire Facebook Marketing Cheat Sheet" to close out the blog post. You want every article that you publish and pro-mote to have these "trapdoors"/links in the text. This is why having a dozen or more lead magnets is important. That way you can include a relevant one every single time you publish new content.

Once you establish your lead magnets be sure that you continue to add new ones and don't skimp on how many different landing pages and offers you have. Here's why, per Hubspot's benchmark data from over seven thousand businesses, "business websites with 10-15 landing pages increase conversions by 55% over business websites with less than 10 landing pages. And those with more than 40 landing pages increase conversions by over 500%." More angles, more offers, more ideas, and more lead magnets on landing pages means more leads and conversions.

OPTIMIZING YOUR CONTENT FOR SOCIAL MEDIA

Optimizing your content for social media is another important part of the code. While lead generation optimization is about ensuring your content works on people and search engine optimization placates the algorithms that rank pages, social media optimization is a hybrid of both. You've got to appeal to the human mind as well as the machines that determine how visible your posts were. Thankfully, there is some crossover in what these two distinct groups like.

Let's start with the importance of visuals when optimizing your content for social media.

Software Advice teamed up with Adobe to conduct the first ever "Social Media Content Optimization Survey."[2] They wanted to "better understand what tactics marketers use to optimize social media content." The key findings from the survey revealed the top tactics used when optimizing social media content. Here they are, with my take on why each is so important:

- **Using images and photos is the most important tactic for optimizing content for social media.** This one is a no-brainer and something you should consider with every post to every social network. In fact, you need an "image is everything" mind-set with social media content. We don't read our feeds— we skim them. It is *much* easier to grab someone's attention in a crowded newsfeed or Twitter stream with images than it is with plain text. As an example, if you are sharing a link to a blog post on Facebook, Twitter, or LinkedIn, be sure an *amazing* picture pulls through into the newsfeed. No matter what you share or where you share it, make it *look* great. If you don't, it won't matter how much time you spent writing it, because no one will be reading it. When we go over Facebook ads (page 48) you will hear this advice again.
- **Using hashtags and specific usernames when sharing.** Using popular hashtags and tagging power social media users are the next best ways to optimize content for search. You can use Hashtracking.com to find popular hashtags and then use them when you post to Facebook, Twitter, or Instagram. This gets your content beyond the feeds of just your followers. It is

also helpful to use tags and mentions strategically. If you share something you think someone else would like and may also share, tag them on Facebook or add a "cc" with their Twitter handle to the end of your Tweet.

- **Targeting specific groups or users**: There are a ton of Facebook Groups, blogs and Twitter accounts that are large, active, and built around a singular topic, like being a mom. Try to find and identify the admins of these Groups and accounts, and then create content that would be impossible for them not to share with their community. You can use the search bar at the top of Facebook and search "Groups about X" or "Groups so and so is in" as ways to discover popular Groups. Or use Klout.com/explore to find the most influential people online, by topic or keyword.

Sharing Is Caring (and it works)

Of course, much of the goal of all these optimization tips is more clicks. But we also want more shares so that our messages are then brought by our inner circle to their inner circles. You definitely want to have social share buttons on all of your blog posts. BrightEdge Technologies studied the top 10,000 websites for its "Social-Share Analysis: Tracking Social Adoption and Trends."[3] When it came to Twitter, they analyzed 4 million tweets and found that "On average, a website without a Twitter share button was mentioned four times, while a site with a tweet button was mentioned 27 times. Including a Twitter plugin button increased mentions on Twitter almost sevenfold."

There are very few things you can do in marketing that get a 7x increase in performance. AddThis and ShareThis are both great services that allow you to add social sharing to your site in seconds. They also allow you to customize the look and feel to match your site's design and are mobile optimized. The social networks themselves also provide "native" buttons for Like, Share, Tweet, Follow, Subscribe, and so forth. Make sure you include the social share options that are best for your audience. I am a fan of including only the critical social sharing icons over having every possible sharing option. You can pick up thousands of additional visitors, page views, and leads using these tools. AddThis and ShareThis both provide detailed analytics so that you can see how the shares are impacting your site and the size of your social following.

Not only can following these best practices help you capture more leads, they can also help you *convert* more of the relationships and leads you already have. The survey findings show that "optimizing social media content is most effective for nurturing relationships." This may refer to relationships with existing customers, or to those leads in the middle stage of the sales funnel. While email marketing (covered on page 95) is the more traditional method for lead nurturing, personalized social media content can be used to achieve the same outcome.

Optimizing Your Content for Google

You want to create content in a way that Google sees it and then positions it as highly as possible. Honestly, just following the "perfect" blog post directions from the last chapter is half the SEO battle.

But with the Facebook marketing (page 37) and email marketing tips you will learn later in the code, the nice thing for salespeople and marketers is that you do not *need* Google or SEO to be successful online anymore.

With each of the ventures I have been a part of where the sales teams had an endless supply of good leads to call (like you will have by the end of this section), SEO was never a primary acquisition channel. Why? SEO is passive lead generation. It is demand fulfillment. And it is way more competitive and expensive than Facebook right now. Sure, there is a huge upside to getting found at the "zero moment of truth" in Google, but it is still a passive play because it is predicted on the user actively searching. Demand generation, direct response marketing, and social media advertising are the future of lead generation, not SEO.

Now I am not denying that SEO can be huge for a business, but it can also feel like a daunting, almost impossible mission for nontechnical folks. As an example: even if a local real estate agent *nailed* SEO and did everything right, making every change Google made from Penguin to Panda, they would still have a hard time outranking Zillow or Trulia for highly searched, valuable keywords.

When I started my first blog, I never once thought about search engines. I wrote only things that I knew my audience would love. Inevitably, much of what I wrote had strategic keywords in it. As an example, if I published a blog post entitled "Best iPad Apps for Real Estate Agents" and then I promoted the article on my Facebook page and to my email list, I quickly found myself ranking for Google searches with the same keywords. Imagine that.

When it comes to optimizing your content for search, don't overthink it. I provide a great checklist ahead that you can use as a framework, but to break it down to the very basics, the "secret sauce" is simply to crank out great content, call it what it is, optimize it, promote it through email and social, then maybe make some final tweaks, and move on. When I say "call it what it is" I am referring to not getting too cute if you want to rank highly in the SERPs (search engine results pages). In my prior example of the article about the iPad apps I could have called it, "You Will LOVE to Touch These Hot New iPad Apps." This could have resulted in some additional social sharing due to a clever title, but the long-term indexing of that post would not bring me relevant visitors through Google for years to come like "Best iPad Apps for Real Estate Agents" did.

Quick Sprout recently published "The Ultimate SEO Checklist: 25 Questions to Ask Yourself before Your Next Post."[4] While the entire list is worth reading, here are the ones they listed that I would con-cur are a "must-do" based on effectiveness, but also based on ease of implementation. I've included how I personally do each one:

- **Research**: I use Google Trends, the Google Keyword Planner, and SEM Rush to quickly identify what words I should use as my primary keywords. I do this immediately AFTER I have the idea for the article. So if I were considering writing an article about iPad applications, these tools help me quickly decide if I should use the word "applications" or the word "apps," if I should use the word "iPad," or if I should use the word "tablet," and so forth.
- **Cross linking**: I try to link every article I have written to another article I have written that was in the same genre/category. On-site links are important for Google to see that you are the authority on a topic, not just someone who wrote about it once. Try putting the links to related articles in the text of your blog posts and more specifically put the links to the other posts in the keywords you want to rank for.
- **Headline**: Google will usually display the first 55 characters in a headline. The headline is the H1 tag and also typical in the URL structure and thus has the most weight for SEO when you publish a post.
- **First 100 words**: You just learned in the last chapter that story-telling can REALLY increase your time on-site. Be sure to also use keywords in your "story" when you can. The first 100 words or so are what Google will also display in the SERPS below the title of the page or post.
- **Subheadline**: This is where you want to take advantage of H2 and H3 tags. Per Buffer, "these tags are signifying a content's importance both to the reader and to search engines. We use H1 headings for our headlines and H2 and H3 headings for the subheads inside each story ... even go(ing) an extra step to bold the subheads to make them really stand out."

  What I love about H2 tags is that they are good for the reader AND the search engines, which is pretty rare. For the article with the headline "Best iPad Apps for Real Estate Agents," the subheadline/H2 tag could have been "Great mobile applications real estate agents can download today." Now instead of Google picking up only words like "best," "iPad," and "apps," they can also more easily pick up "great," "mobile," "applications," and "download." Think about synonyms when you do this. Simply repeating the headline is not the best way to go for the reader or the search engines for your subheadline.

- **Outbound links to related blogs:** I also try to include at least one link to another website that isn't mine in each post I write. This gives Google a better idea of who you are, what other sites are related to yours, and what additional keywords it should be considering you for.

Don't worry about sending people away from your site (when it happens). The more you send people away to additional great resources, the more they will come back. Plus, Google likes links to places other than *only* your other pages and posts.

So you have a website and landing pages built for lead capture. You've drafted a few perfect blog posts. Your content is optimized for lead generation, social media, and search engines. You can now start sending people to your online assets *with confidence* knowing that many will be "converted."

Advanced Facebook Marketing and Advertising Techniques That Generate "Ready to Buy" Leads

A key component of The Conversion Code is social media, which I most often refer to as "Facebook, plus everything else." Facebook has become our home screen of the Internet. In August 2015, Mark Zuckerberg announced that 1 billion people used Facebook in the same day. Think about that for a second. One in seven people on earth were all on the same website in the same 24-hour period.

In findings published by parse.ly, July 2015 marked the first time that Facebook sent more traffic to news sites than Google. Per *Fortune*, "The company's clients include more than 400 major news and media outlets, including traditional publishers such as Wired, The Atlantic, Reuters and The Daily Telegraph, as well as a large group of digital-only outlets such as Mashable, The Next Web, and Business Insider."[1]

Of all the powerful statistics about Facebook one could gather, this one really is a Gladwell-esque "tipping point." Why? We are not only addicted to the content created by our friends and family so much that we look at Facebook more than we look at each other in the face (we already knew that), but we *also* now turn to our network as a filter of other people and companies' content. This isn't about me trusting my friends from high school more than I trust Google. It is about me trusting that my network at large has already found so many interesting things without me having to search that I start at Facebook, not Google. I start with trust. Find is the new search. And you can have amazing ads interwoven into that fabric of established trust and addiction....

REFERRAL TRAFFIC FROM GOOGLE VERSUS FACEBOOK

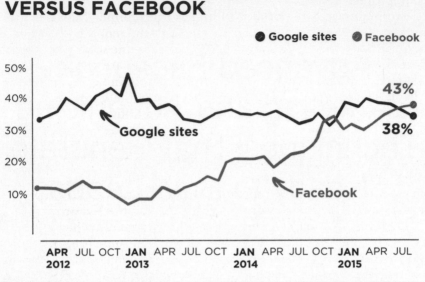

Figure 4.1

My six-year-old daughter tells me to "look it up on Facebook" or "post that on Instagram" all the time. She has never asked me to "Google" something or to "pull up" a website. Google, PPC, SEO, and the other social networks matter. It's just that Facebook matters the most.

But despite this overwhelming evidence, it is being greatly underutilized as a purposeful, consistent, and quality lead generation source. How underutilized? As of February 2015, there were only 2 million advertisers on Facebook. Two billion users, 2 million advertisers...

When you go deeper into the number of advertisers that are doing it right, there is certainly even less competition. So in this chapter of *The Conversion Code* I will teach you how to leverage the New Internet (Facebook) to capture leads every single day. I'm going to start with the things that you can do today, for free, on Facebook to generate leads.

FACEBOOK PROFILE PRO TIPS

Even if you never run a Facebook ad, never start a Facebook page, or never admin a Facebook group (all of which I will teach ahead), at a minimum you should be able to generate leads from your Facebook profile.

Authenticity is important. People want to connect, not feel marketed to, when they accept your Facebook friend request. Believe it or not, your day-to-day life should be the number-one source of inspiration for content and updates on Facebook. What are you doing that's interesting? Right now you are reading an awesome book about converting leads, as an example. Take a picture of the book and share it on Facebook right now with the hashtag #TheConversionCode.

The best Facebook marketers are the ones who are willing to share genuine moments of their lives, the good and the bad. When it comes to Facebook profiles, lurkers lose. Consistency matters. You need to be either semi-interesting daily or really interesting weekly, at a minimum. You can't expect to hop onto Facebook once a month and share what is happening in your life and get any traction or business from it.

You need to first start by understanding exactly what and why Facebook puts into their users' newsfeed. Each morning when you wake up and check Facebook, it is not an accident what appears on your screen. Similar to Google's infamous Page Rank formula, Facebook also uses a highly complex algorithm referred to as Edge Rank to determine what gets seen and what doesn't. If you want your status updates to be interacted with, clicked on, and ultimately send you leads, it is critical that you get it seen. The algorithm around why users see what seems to apply pretty equally to what and how you share things on profiles and pages.

Here are the top four reasons why we see what we see in our Facebook newsfeeds:

1. How popular are the posts you've made in the past? If your past posts typically get Likes and comments, Facebook will give you the benefit of the doubt on your new posts.
2. How popular is the post with the people who have seen it? Think of this as Facebook doing a quick test of your post with a small group of your friends. Based on those initial interactions with it, Facebook either shows the post more or less often to other users.
3. How popular are your posts with that specific person? The one-to-one relationships you build on Facebook are important. Beyond just how popular your average posts are, Facebook also looks at the micro level of how popular your posts are with each of your friends individually.
4. What type of post does each particular user like the most? I personally click on a lot of links, so Facebook makes sure I get lots of links and articles in my newsfeed. If you're a person who

"Likes" check-ins or pictures more, you'll see more check-in and photo posts.

Based on these findings, here is my advice for reaching a broad audience: Post highly interesting shit and vary your post types. The segments of your audience have different browsing habits and tendencies, so you should share some posts with pictures, some with videos, some with links, and so forth. While you may prefer links or videos, what your friends prefer is also heavily weighted as to what they will be shown. Bottom line? Be interesting, be consistent, and be diverse with what you post.

Where Can You Find Great Content for Sharing Using Your Facebook Profile?

Outside of your personal and professional life, there are some great additional ways to find things that are "share worthy" on Facebook. Oddly enough, my number-one place to find things to share with my community on Facebook is Twitter. Taking your time and building a Twitter list of reporters, media outlets, and bloggers can really pay you back day after day. It might take you some time to build the list, but once it is up, you can check it all day, every day for things your FB friends probably haven't seen yet. Twitter moves *much* faster than Facebook, so often you can bring "breaking news" from Twitter to Facebook and be the first one sharing it.

Even if you do not use Twitter, what I am really doing here is waking up, reading what I love, and then sharing things I read with those who will also love it. This could be the morning paper or my favorite blog, not just a Twitter list. The point is you are already consuming content every day. Just turn the corner and start sharing it, too.

Three other great sources for finding interesting, shareable content for your Facebook profile are BuzzSumo, Upworthy, and ViralNova. In short, you don't have to *create* content to be great on Facebook. Curation can work as well. The key is to be consistent. If you post eight or nine highly engaging and interesting items you curated, then you post one you created, the posts you shared that were curated assist in how many people will see your original content.

Timing and Frequency That Get the Maximum Impact for Your Facebook Posts

Beyond diversifying the content you share, the timing and frequency of your sharing can also have a dramatic impact on metrics like reach and engagement. Set Up a Blog Today published an infographic enti-tled "The Science of Posting on Social Media" which provided best practices around frequency and timing for all of the most popular social networks.[2] Here is what they found to be the "best" for Face-book. I put best in quotes because there are no universal truths here. The reality is that the person who is right now the most likely to buy from you could be checking Facebook at 3:00 A.M. and willing to click only on posts with videos. Regardless of the anomalies that will occur, the following advice is spot-on:

- Posting once a week is not enough, but posting more than once a day is semi-annoying (citing a 2011 Socialbakers study).
- Best time to post for getting click-throughs is 1 to 4 P.M. (this makes sense as we have gotten some work done, had lunch, and can now check Facebook more deeply). Wednesday at 3 P.M. (hump day, anyone?) was the peak time/day combo.
- Worst time to post for click-throughs was on the weekends before 8 A.M. and after 8 P.M.

Social media is not that different than regular media in the ways that people check it out. There are segments on Facebook that are "morning people" (these people probably watch the morning news). There are those on Facebook who are "night owls" (these people prob-ably watch the evening news).

One semi-scientific way I have found to calculate *your* peak time for posting is to keep an eye on the number of your friends that are currently available on live chat. Take note of the days and times when that number is at its highest and its lowest. This should be a solid indi-cator as to when the most people in your network would see an update.

Thanks, Chris, I Appreciate That

There is a lot of power in using someone's name when interacting on Facebook (and social media in general), yet very few people do it. When you address someone and use their name, it feels more per-sonal. It may be a small thing, but that's an important part of the lesson: All these small things add up to the big thing.

We use people's names when addressing them almost everywhere, but we don't on social media. We do it on letters, in emails, and on the phone. But rarely do we say when commenting on Facebook. "Looks like you are having a blast on vacation, Steve!" Compare that to "Looks like you guys are having a blast on vacation!" and you can immedi-ately feel the difference.

Another small thing I do that shows people I am listening to them and that I care is to Like or reply back with a comment on every comment someone leaves on my posts. If they leave an in-depth, well-thought-out comment, I reply in the same vein. If they leave a quick comment, I at least hit Like on it to let them know I read it. Facebook is like tennis: It's pretty boring when only one person is playing.

HBD = WTF

Have you ever had someone take the time to write HBD on your wall for your birthday? Wow, thanks. You spent all of three characters on me . . . When someone does that to me, three more characters come to mind: WTF. While Facebook makes it easy to write on someone's wall for their birthday, think outside the box. Hundreds of other people are likely doing the exact same thing. When I see that it is someone's birthday on Facebook, I actually mail them a handwritten note (I love using Bond.co for these). I always include my cell phone and email address below my signature. Time and time again, I get a THANK YOU message immediately upon it hitting their mailbox. I have even seen people *post* a picture of the card I mailed them.

Get More Comments, Right Now

I'm going to show you a magic trick.

Update your Facebook status right now. Ask your friends, "How many states have you lived in?"

There is a good chance that by the time you finish this chapter, your post will have more comments than any that you've ever made. Not Likes. Comments. Which weigh more heavily into how Facebook determines what to show next. The reason? That post is something that I call "built for social." It's something anyone can answer in one second with two buttons (their answer and post).

When you use social media to ask why, it can take deep thought. More thought than most people will give in our microwave-mentality, :08 attention span world. When you ask when, or who, or how many, it takes a lot less brainpower to respond. Best of all, when you ask simple, easy-to-answer questions, you're going to learn interesting things about your network.

Zillow does a great job of this with their Facebook business page. Every week, they run a post called "Taste Test Tuesday." They put two homes side by side in an image. The homes are listed at the same price. All they do is ask which of the two you'd rather have. Countless comments come pouring in.

A or B? Yes or no? How many? Not hard questions to answer. On Facebook, the calls to action that work are the ones that play well within their established ecosystem.

The 3-3 Facebook Time Blocking Technique

You need to block time off each day (at least Monday through Friday) to make authentic, but scalable, connections on Facebook. I call it "the 3-3 Technique," and it can be a game changer for your business. The timing of these messages is not as critical as the timing of a status update, but before we dive in let me make it very clear that the 3-3 Technique works *much* better if the person is currently logged onto Facebook. The easiest way to know that is to look at your Facebook Chat tool.

What's the 3-3 Technique? Like I said before, lurkers lose. So log into Facebook with an active mentality and a plan. The 3-3 Technique consists of doing these two things without fail:

1. Write on three of your friends' walls each day. Most people use Facebook only as a "one to many" tool. I use Facebook as a one-to-one tool (that many can still luckily see). When you write on someone's wall, they get alerted instantly. They don't when you simply update your status. These are your colleagues, classmates, friends, and family, so it shouldn't be too hard to "drop by" and make three people each day feel special. I will often leave a link to an article I know they will love or sometimes I just pop by and write, "Hope you are well. Let's catch up soon!" Try it right now. I guarantee you will get some conversations going, today.

2. Start three private Facebook chats each day. Again, just updating your status is not enough. People open and read their Facebook messages at an even higher clip than they read their actual email. If you are not using Facebook's inbox you are really missing out. I will usually make the private messages a little bit more about business (without being spammy). I usually just send something like "Hey, I am working on a big project for work—can I pick your brain?" Use these messages to get on the phone with your network!

There are about 260 weekdays in a year. With the 3-3 Technique, even though you are reaching only six people per workday, over the course of one year you will have sent 1,560 "one-to-one" messages! I cannot convey how important this is to growing your network, generating inbound leads, getting referrals, and crushing it on Facebook.

People Are Sharing—Here Is One Clever Way to Show You Care

Another great strategy for going above and beyond using your Facebook profile is "the Alex Wang Strategy." Alex is a real estate agent in Palo Alto, and he noticed that many of his colleagues and network share on Facebook when they are on a vacation, usually uploading dozens of photos and albums of their trip. Alex actually does something special for them *while* they are on vacation. How can you make their experience better? Instead of "Hey, it's been a year since we worked together, how have you been!" upgrade their travel experience, send wine to their room (if they like wine), or maybe you could check out the highest-rated restaurants near where they are staying on Yelp and send them a gift card. Bottom line? As Paul Graham, founder of Y Combinator, once famously said (and what Alex Wang is executing), "Do things that don't scale."

Rebumping Old Posts

I am sure at one point you have commented on someone's post, only to be bombarded with notifications that others were doing the same. Facebook's notifications can be very powerful when used to your advantage. One thing you can do right now to stir up some instant engagement is to go back to your old popular posts and "rebump" them. Basically, you add another comment like "I was rereading all of these nice comments today and it made me smile." This will cause Facebook to immediately notify some of those who had previously Liked or commented on the post. Even if the post is several years old, this seems to hold true. Facebook actually makes this easy with their "on this day" feature which highlights your most engaging posts from the past.

One clever tactic is to create a blog post related to those super popular posts after the fact. Then you can go back to the lengthy thread and say, "You all inspired me to dig deeper on this topic so I just published an article: LINK."

Comments Are King

Even if you do not update your status each day, inevitably your network is updating theirs. One simple best practice for getting your edge rank up and increasing your Facebook presence is to live in the comments. Comment on 25 people's posts per day. I use a Facebook list called my "MVC" (Most Valuable Connections). By taking the time to set them all up on one list, I can see just what they are sharing, which makes commenting much easier and quicker to do. How do you determine who your MVCs are? Ask yourself this question: Of your Facebook connections, who are the 25 percent who matter the most to your business? Put them on their own list and check it like crazy. But don't just lurk! Leave comments. *Live in the comments.* You should be commenting on other people's Facebook posts 10 to 100 times more often than you are updating your status.

Also, with the way email notifications and default settings work, commenting (across ALL social media platforms) is much more likely to trigger a message being sent to them than simply liking their posts will.

FACEBOOK GROUPS

Facebook groups are probably THE most underutilized tool on Facebook. I have been an admin of groups with 20,000+ members for years now, and it is a consistent driver of traffic, leads, and sales. You have to think bigger than just a Facebook profile and page (which I will cover ahead). You need to also build a Facebook group around an idea, not around your brand.

Our Facebook groups are called Tech Support Group for Real Estate Agents and What Should I Spend My Money On? These topics are related to what we sell, but it was a purposeful decision not to start "The Chris Smith/Curaytor Fan Club." Don't get me wrong, we do also use a secret Facebook group for our paid client-only Mastermind. But by having these bigger groups that are help focused we get traffic leads and sales from Facebook groups while most companies are ONLY using groups for support and service.

I sincerely recommend that you ask yourself the following question before starting a Facebook group: Will this group be relevant five years from now and will I want to wake up every day and post to it? We felt that agents would still need tech support and still have questions about their spending five years from now, and we know that we will still love technology and helping people, so we did it.

A good example of how a focused group can take off is to look at nextdoor.com, a social network for neighborhoods. People connecting with other people on a local level—it's focused on a specific/well-defined community. You should be the nextdoor.com for your niche, using a Facebook group instead—go knock on doors and make flyers/mailers as invitations to join the group. If you are a national brand, follow our lead and be *the* go-to resource for help on Facebook. The sales will follow. Gary Vaynerchuk calls it "The Thank You Economy." The more times you give someone on Facebook a reason to say "thanks," the more likely they are to share your stuff, buy from you down the road, or even refer people to you.

You can't be the only one posting in your group. But you also can't expect it to take off right away. Find folks who will contribute and be ambassadors early on; the more contributors you have, the more your group will spread in a grassroots way. Plus, groups need strong admins and group guidelines so they do not get overrun with spam and self-promotion (by others).

When done right, it becomes a culture. It becomes bigger than you, so make it special. As an example, we have a custom header image, stating our group's purpose, rules, and admins. These small touches can lead to big growth. There are plenty of little things that you can do to make your Facebook group take off: Change the URL of your group (you do this by changing the email address of your group). I'd even recommend buying a unique, non-Facebook URL for the group, and then have it forward to the group page. As an example: WarrenGroup.com is much better for mailers, business cards, and just saying out loud versus having to print or say, "Go to facebook.com/group/7472548."

*A quick pro tip is that **anytime** you are using a* Facebook.com *URL in your marketing, you can actually just use* FB.com. *You can see it in action right now by visiting* FB.com/CuraytorChris, *which will open up my Facebook page (feel free to Like it while you are there and write on my wall to let me know you just read this). Sometimes the full URL with Facebook spelled out and your custom ending can be too long for print or to make look nice when designing collateral.*

You will also need to decide between an open, closed, or secret group. Those choices are pretty straightforward. Open groups can be seen and read by users who haven't joined. Closed can't. Secret you can't find. Open groups grow the fastest, but attract the most spam and can keep people from truly "telling all." Closed groups allow for more candid conversations, but grow slowly because nonmembers cannot see the threads without joining. Secret groups I keep super small and focused, like our Curaytor client-only Mastermind, where all we do is talk shop.

How do you find people to join your group? Use Facebook search to find popular, well-run groups your friends are already in and target groups with similar interests. As an example, you could search for "What groups is Mark Zuckerberg in?" If during this search you end up finding groups that are already doing what you're wanting to do, get active in those! Provide value. You don't have to start your own group. I have seen countless members of my groups begin to also get business and referrals by being helpful, consistently.

Either way, whether you start your own group or join and contribute to others, you should be a part of groups around your passion/purpose. This will keep you engaged, over time.

FACEBOOK PAGES

The most common question I get from business owners is what's best for drumming up business on Facebook: profiles or pages? The answer is yes. They all work great, if you work them. Conversations lead to appointments and referrals; appointments and referrals lead to sales. Conversations create conversions. Facebook creates conversations.

Here is the #1 reason you 100 percent *must* have a Facebook page to crack The Conversion Code: You cannot run Facebook ads without a Facebook page. And what you will learn ahead about setting up a Facebook ad funnel is not an optional part of the code.

Often, people overlook the design of their Facebook page. Pimp your page out—make it look amazing. Your profile pic that you choose for your page will be in the ads you run, so choose wisely. Your cover pic should be spectacular and updated regularly. Your bio and information tabs should be filled out thoroughly. Think of your Facebook page as your backup website. Obsess about every detail during the setup and optimization phases. Most of the best practices for posting I mentioned earlier regarding your profile also apply to pages. But your "fans" and your "friends" will likely have different tastes.

Tools like SumoRank, LikeAlyzer, and Facebook Insights are great for quickly seeing how your page has been performing, plus what it can do better and how it ranks against others in your industry. My favorite thing about these tools is that they work for *any* Facebook page, not just yours. This is a *great* way to see what your competition is up to that is working well.

I also highly recommend that if you are going to be running a Facebook page, you learn the parts of Facebook Insights that can help you tremendously. I use Insights for two primary reasons. First, I use the Pages to Watch feature to spy on my competition as well as other pages I admire that are nicely run to see how we are comparing to them. Setting this up only takes a minute, and once it is done you can see what is shown in Figure 4.2 at any time.

The second way I use Insights is to find out which of my posts work the best. The goal of The Conversion Code is to drive traffic to a place where we can capture their information. So with that in mind, I am mostly looking for the posts that got the most post clicks. You can sort every post you have ever done by Reach or Engagement (see Figure 4.3).

Page			Total Page Likes	From Last Week	Posts This Week	Engagement This Week
1		National Association of ...	225.1K	▲0.4%	26	9.3K
2		Top Producer Systems	47.2K	▲0.5%	3	10
3		Tech Savvy Agent	34.2K	0%	1	15
4		Real Estate Trends	20.5K	0%	0	0

Figure 4.2

Reach: Organic / Paid ▼   Post Clicks Likes, Comments & Shares ▼

Published	Post		Type	Targeting	Reach	Engagement		Promote
07/16/2015 2:23 pm		Chris and Jimmy JUST announced their first ever real estate conference!! Here is a special audio m	🔗	🌐	7.6K	150 190		Boost Post
08/27/2015 1:55 pm		Our co-founder Chris Smith was just featured in T he Huffington Post for his advice on internet lead	🖼	🌐	1.1K	98 15		Boost Post
06/25/2015 3:52 pm		We were pumped to see Curaytor mentioned in th is new article about the future of online ad spend i	🔗	🌐	3.7K	70 82		Boost Post

Figure 4.3

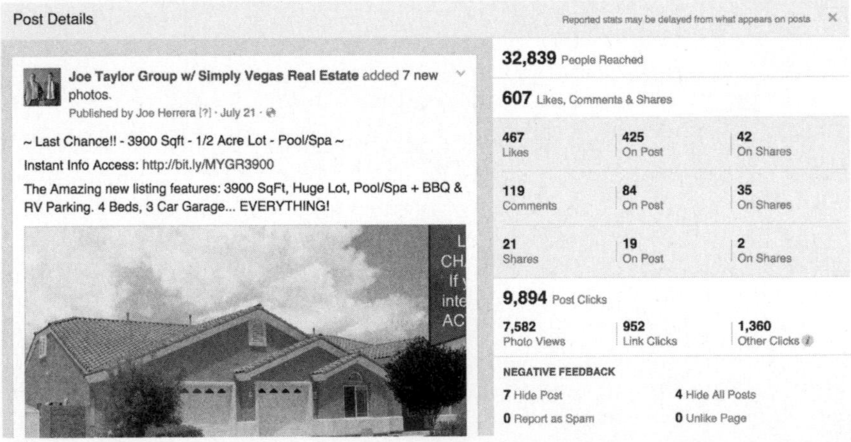

Post Details   Reported stats may be delayed from what appears on posts   ✕

Joe Taylor Group w/ Simply Vegas Real Estate added 7 new photos.
Published by Joe Herrera [?] · July 21 · 🌐

~ Last Chance!! - 3900 Sqft - 1/2 Acre Lot - Pool/Spa ~
Instant Info Access: http://bit.ly/MYGR3900

The Amazing new listing features: 3900 SqFt, Huge Lot, Pool/Spa + BBQ & RV Parking. 4 Beds, 3 Car Garage... EVERYTHING!

32,839 People Reached

607 Likes, Comments & Shares

467 Likes	**425** On Post	**42** On Shares
119 Comments	**84** On Post	**35** On Shares
21 Shares	**19** On Post	**2** On Shares

9,894 Post Clicks

7,582 Photo Views	**952** Link Clicks	**1,360** Other Clicks ⓘ

NEGATIVE FEEDBACK

7 Hide Post	4 Hide All Posts
0 Report as Spam	0 Unlike Page

Figure 4.4

I also like to look at the micro-level data from each post that did well to see what elements may have contributed to that. As you start to identify the best posts with the most clicks, post more updates like those moving forward.

For posts that you boost with an ad, you can see this data in Ads Manager or Power Editor (more on both below). But Insights is where you can see every post, ad or not. When you are in Facebook Insights and you pull up any post, it will give you a detailed analysis of the post (see Figure 4.4).

FACEBOOK ADS

Over the last seven years, I have run and managed millions of dollars in Facebook advertising spend. Two things I know as fact based on this experience: (1) Facebook ads got a lot better once the company went public, and (2) Facebook cares enough about their users that they come up with ways to help advertisers reach them in the most relevant and effective ways possible.

Facebook ads are so powerful they can quickly make a good business great or a great business excellent. Technology is an *accelerator* of greatness. When I started using Facebook ads, I was already the number-one salesperson in my channel at Move Inc. I didn't *need* more leads or sales. But I was *great* at what I did offline. So when I transferred my knowledge to the web, using a Facebook page, Facebook ads, a WordPress blog, and YouTube Channel to start, my new audience liked what I had to say, in the same ways that my local audience had.

If the only thing that you do after reading this book is build a Facebook ad funnel for your business, it alone can produce enough leads to keep nearly any sales team busy and will increase your sales. Remember, Facebook is the New Internet. Don't go into Facebook ads looking to supplement what you are doing online. Go into it with the mind-set that it can become your #1 channel for traffic, leads, and sales. Anything less is a user error. I am giving you the exact blueprint.

What Facebook ads *can't* do: They can't make a bad business good. And if you're an established business, you probably won't triple your sales overnight—so think big, but also be realistic. This is mostly due to the fact that Facebook ads can't close a lead. They can only get you hot leads consistently. Facebook ads simply put the ball on the tee. It's up to the batter (salesperson) to hit the ball. That is why the entire third section of *The Conversion Code* is dedicated to how to close a lead over the phone. Zuck ain't doing that for you!

Before we get into the strategies and tactics required to fill your funnel, it is important to note the differences between Google and Facebook ads.

Google is in the business of demand fulfillment. Their user showed intent by keying in a certain phrase, and Google can display your ad at this very critical moment. Certainly, this makes sense and has proven to be effective as a lead generation channel for those who got it right. However, the reason The Conversion Code relies more on Facebook ads than Google ads is simple.

Demand Generation Is Greater Than Demand Fulfillment

For the first time, a website besides Google has so much scale, time on site, and engagement that you can have your ad in front of your dream customer BEFORE they ever even perform a Google search.

Imagine taking a quick look at Google Trends and learning about the search traffic for a certain phrase, like "July 4th fireworks." You'd be unsurprised to see that this traffic spikes on the 1st, 2nd, and 3rd of July. Why not go into Facebook and place an ad in everyone's news-feed on June 29 and 30 with the same message linked to a blog post with the answer? How many people would you stop from ever even searching?

So that's the good news. You can now create demand without buying traditional media. Which means any business can play the game. The bad news is that with Facebook ads, you need to be much more creative and strategic than you ever had to be with search engine marketing or pay-per-click. This is largely due to the visual nature of Facebook ads. With Google PPC, it is all about nailing the search terms, copy, and where you send the click. Clever copywriting and optimized landing pages matter with Facebook ads, too, but the biggest difference is how much more image-centric Facebook ads are than Google. Sure, you can use Google's display network to put banner ads all over the Internet, but Facebook newsfeed ads are much more "native" in design and relevant when targeted and deployed properly.

Don't have a huge budget, but have huge ambitions? Facebook ads are a blank, cheap canvas for you to paint on. Facebook ads can produce champagne results on a beer budget. Especially if you have ever dabbled in the costly world of traditional advertising.

Real estate agents and lawyers have tried to portray themselves as being larger than life for years. They often did this by purchasing big billboards or bus benches. Facebook ads are the new billboard. And the nice thing is that this billboard is seen by only the perfect people. Not by every car that drives down the interstate. And you don't even have to pay for the billboard being seen—you pay only when someone *you* identified as the perfect client clicks on your billboard.

Ahead I will cover the essentials of great Facebook ads, the four types of Facebook ads every business should run, and how to target your ideal customer.

THE ESSENTIALS OF RUNNING A GREAT FACEBOOK AD

No matter what kind of Facebook ad you decide to run, no matter who you decide to target, whether you use Power Editor, Ads Manager, or a boosted post, no matter your methodology, there are critical essentials to EVERY Facebook ad you will run.

Image Is Everything (Canon Cameras and Andre Agassi got it right)

What would it look like if the only thing your Facebook ad had was the image? Do you notice text when you're scrolling through your newsfeed on your phone? Probably not nearly at the clip that you see images. Start every Facebook ad with a killer image, and then work backwards. When you create a Facebook ad, try creating it with the mentality that the image in the ad is the entire ad.

I have found that images or custom-designed ad pieces with white/negative space and bright colors mixed in perform great. In fact, the brighter the colors or image, the better the results. Dark, dull images get terrible click-through rates compared to bright, bold images. While analyzing some internal data at Curaytor, I discovered that campaigns we managed featuring professional photos of homes produced a 3x higher CTR versus those using amateur or cell phone photos.

When I say, "Image is everything," there's another image that everyone forgets about: Your Facebook page profile picture is in nearly every ad you will run. Make sure it looks great in the newsfeed. Sometimes you can't just cram your existing logo into your profile picture. You need an "icon" version of your logo, like what your company's mobile app icon would look like. We reduce Curaytor to just the C on all of our social media profiles.

"Extras" and Text over the Image

Once you nail your ad image, next is adding some text and/or "extras" to the image. By "extras" I mean things like borders, ribbons, buttons, arrows, or even your logo. Remember, keep these additions bright.

Gold, green, red, orange, blue, and purple make for great colors that really pop when sitting on top of Facebook's white interface. I use Picmonkey to quickly add extras, overlays, and text to my images.

Regarding the text you can add, there is a little bad news: You can't have more than 20 percent of the image covered by text. That rule is the bane of my existence sometimes, but I understand why Facebook enforces it. If they didn't, people would just use their business cards or screenshots of their websites as their ads. Or, they would put *huge* words over their images like "BUY NOW" or "ON SALE," which would really hurt the user experience of the platform, making it feel awfully spammy very quickly. What this rule encourages is that instead of trying to squeeze your entire message into the text, the text should instead complement the image and extras. Facebook actually has a handy tool for checking the ratio of text to images before you post.

Believe it or not, all of the things I just covered are only to get the person to stop and read our ad copy.

Killer, Clever Copy

Not everyone will read the words in your post (with a well-crafted image, many will click without reading), but the people who will buy from you will most likely read every word you write. If you're spending less than five minutes on the copy of a Facebook ad, you're not a professional marketer. Sure, Facebook makes it easy to launch and deploy ads, but good things come to those who wait. My dad used to tell me to "think before I speak." His advice applies to Facebook ads. Consider that it may end up costing you thousands of dollars to get your ads in front of and clicked by the right people, so you'll probably want to spend a little time crafting your message.

I literally spend hours talking about the copy for Facebook ads with my team. Run your copy by someone: Double-check your commas and spelling, and make sure there's not an extra space, and so forth. Obsess about what you write, because serious leads are going to read it.

When you write amazing copy, it can also help filter and qualify the leads for you. This can save you a ton of time and money. As an example, if I were a real estate agent running an ad that said, "Check your home's value today!" it would get a lot of clicks and leads. If I ran a comparable ad that read, "Selling your home soon? Check your home's value today!" it would get fewer leads, but they'd be closer to transacting.

At Curaytor, our services are not inexpensive. But most people who hear about what we do want to buy it. So instead of plastering our pricing to keep anyone who can't afford us away (which is a *terrible* idea at our price point, to give your price before you give your value), we use copy like "Exclusively for top-producing salespeople and teams." This both attracts the right leads and repels the wrong ones, all without pissing anyone off.

Specific Calls to Action

Believe it or not, people like to be told what to do. In fact, they need your guidance. Even if your CTA is as simple as "click here to download," "click here to watch this," or "click here to learn more," it is critical that you tell the person reading it *exactly* what the next step is.

If you don't have a strong CTA in your ads, you are wasting your money and asking the people taking the time to read them to do nothing.

As the Facebook lexicon has become part of our everyday vocabulary, a new set of calls to action have also emerged. Asking people to "Like," "Leave a Comment," "Share this Post," or "Tag Someone Below" can be very effective social media–specific calls to action. Because I know how to use Facebook ads so effectively, the events that hire me to speak often ask if I can help them spread the word. When I am going to an area where I do not have a large following, I will ask in the ad for the people I do know to tag anyone they know who may be interested in attending in a comment. Like clockwork, a handful of local people see the ad and tag people from their local network, bringing more awareness to my gig and with the added bonus of a trusted recommendation from a friend!

Mobile Optimized Ads

If you want an endless supply of clicks, leads, and sales from Facebook, you will need to make sure that your ads are being displayed on and optimized for mobile, not just desktop. Facebook (and the world in general) has hit a tipping point where the phone has become the web. Often, images or add-ons or calls to action that look and work great on a large screen are illegible on a phone. There will be times where the images and ads you design will work for both audiences, but there will also be times where you actually need to create two separate sets of ad creatives.

There are certain Facebook ad campaigns where I actually remove all mobile ads and target only desktop users, especially when I am driving them to a more in-depth capture form or landing page. Ads Manager will show you what your ads look like on desktop vs. mobile. I don't do a full registration landing page form on ads I target only on mobile. When I build landing pages I know will be used on mobile,

I just focus on getting email and/or phone only. If a prospective lead has to scroll on their mobile device to complete a landing page form, there is a good chance that will stop them from doing it. Just ask yourself whether you would fill that out if you were in the line at Starbucks, checked Facebook, and then clicked on a post. If there are 10 fields to complete, probably not. So use "light registration" when possible on mobile ad campaigns and landing pages.

This best practice applies to Twitter, YouTube, and Instagram ads, too. If you want to go from a tweet to a lead, you aren't going to get them to spend five minutes filling stuff out when they just came from a 140-character universe. (I'll have more advice for you about Twitter, YouTube, Instagram, and other networks in the next chapter, beginning on page 65.)

A Link to a Proven Mousetrap

By optimizing your website and landing pages the way I taught you earlier, grabbing a link for your Facebook ad that will capture leads will be a one-second process. This is why compelling lead magnets, well-designed landing pages, and a lead generation–optimized website/blog are so important.

Virtually every Facebook ad that we will run will be focused on getting clicks. These clicks cost money. So you need to be sure that a certain percentage of the clicks will indeed become a lead. What's nice is that once you have your links established, you can change everything about a Facebook ad but still link to the same place as a previous ad. At Curaytor, our sales page does a great job at converting qualified leads. That means my job as a marketer is to get people there regularly, and there is more than one way to skin that cat. When I come up with a new Facebook ad, I often link to an old landing page, so I can create separate Facebook ads for the various things that we do, but drive them all to our sales page.

In a perfect world, each ad would get a new landing page, but that's not always necessary. Instead of always building new landing pages, spend as much time or more coming up with new and creative Facebook ads to get people to them.

It is *much* easier to develop and launch a new Facebook ad campaign than it is to build and launch a new landing page.

THE PERFECT FACEBOOK AD FUNNEL

The Conversion Code is built on my C^3 formula of Capturing leads, Creating appointments, and Closing sales. Facebook ads are another part of the code where C^3 is used. In the case of Facebook ads, though, C^3 stands for Content marketing, Conversion marketing, and Closing marketing. Once you identify what you'll be linking to and which of the three buckets each ad falls into, these three Cs start to create a perfect Facebook ad funnel. Then you will also identify the three audiences to target with your ads.

C^3 Facebook Ads

Top Layer—Content Marketing. The Facebook ads that will get the most clicks and engagement will be your content marketing ads. These should link to quality blog posts, videos, or podcasts—anything that entices a ton of clicks and that someone can access without registering. Our goal with these ads is not necessarily to capture leads. Instead we are trying to get anyone with a pulse that might buy from us eventually to visit our site so we can start to build trust and gain brand recognition with them by providing value. This also lets you pixel track them so that you can show them more conversion- and closing-focused Facebook ads through retargeting.

Second Layer—Conversion Marketing. If your business doesn't have enough leads right now (or at least a steady flow of leads each day), you can skip layer one and start with layer two. Your conversion marketing ads will be where you get the highest volume of leads coming in. These ads should link to your lead magnets and landing pages. This layer is where things like offering a guide, e-book, or video to download can work nicely. All of your Facebook conversion marketing ads should link to an offer/capture page.

Bottom Layer—Closing Marketing. Remember, this is a Facebook ad funnel and all of the ads work cohesively. Closing marketing Facebook ads simply account for people moving through the funnel. Closing marketing should be focused on getting your leads to read customer reviews, sign up for a group webinar, schedule a time to speak with sales, call now to learn more, or get a discount by acting now. Your conversion marketing layer consists of all the content you have that lets people know what the next steps are in working together.

The goal and progression of the C^3 Facebook ad funnel are simple. Step 1: Use content marketing to create traffic, awareness, and tracking pixels that trigger more ads. Step 2: Use conversion marketing to better identify who will put their toe in the water by registering and becoming a "lead." Step 3: Use closing marketing as an attempt to make a sale.

A perfect funnel has all three types of ads. But just having the C^3 ads in place is not enough. Now you need to know exactly who to target (and who not to target) with your ads by establishing your three core Facebook ad audiences.

The Three Core Facebook Ad Audiences

You need to create strategic, custom audiences to show your Facebook ads to. Facebook allows for some of the best ad targeting options of all time for marketers, including location, age, education, interests, income, wealth, household composition, and much more. While the possibilities are truly endless when you're cooking up your targeting recipes, make sure at a minimum you develop the following three ad audiences.

1. The Magic Million. This one is simple. Who has a pulse and might buy from you or refer you someone who might buy? Although you may not end up with exactly a million people in this audience, I call it that so you will remember that this audience should be large. As in 100,000, 300,000, or even 1,000,000+ people targeted. The goal is LOTS of people, but factoring in that they "could" to be a paying customer at some point.

A few simple Magic Million audience examples might be a handful of the zip codes you work in. Or to target by several large employers (Nike + Boeing + Ford). Or City + Age. Or State + Age + Education Level. Just be sure not to get too picky here. We need this audience to be large!

I also find that targeting your Magic Million by using Facebook's Interest option can be impactful. As an example, I have an ad audience saved so that I can target people who are interested in Inman News and the three most popular sales coaches in real estate. Just those four interests produce an audience size of over 220,000. While I do not specifically compete with Inman News (a media company) or the coaches (training companies), I do know that their audience is the audience I want to sell my sales and marketing solutions to as well.

Remember, Facebook gives you a tracking pixel that you can install in less than one minute on your website. When somebody from your Magic Million visits a content marketing article (even though you may not require them to register), the next few times they log into Facebook, they will start seeing your conversion marketing ad that does drive them to a capture page. The idea is that you want to build awareness and trust with your Magic Million *before* you ask them for their information or start showing them your more conversion- and closing-focused campaigns.

2. The Chunky Middle.   Anyone from the Magic Million who clicks on a content marketing ad gets automatically added to what I call the Chunky Middle. This happens dynamically thanks to our Facebook tracking pixel being installed on our website. But a Chunky Middle audience also needs to include anyone who Likes your page, your entire email list, and your "dream" audience. You want to target this audience with both your content and conversion-centric ads.

As opposed to the higher-level targeting we used to create the Magic Million, the "dream" targeting here might be somebody 35 to 40, who has owned their home for more than six years, and who loves yoga. Unlike the intended targets of the Magic Million (has pulse, might buy from you), this dream audience segment of your Chunky Middle should be your best possible customers only.

When you add up people who click from the Magic Million, those who Like your page, your current email list, and your dream audience, it can be a lot of people (chunky). This will typically be a decent-sized audience to begin with, but also enables it to continually get "chunkier" by dynamically adding new people to it each day.

Pro tip: Facebook uses the term "Custom Audience" when you upload a CSV file of emails or phone numbers to target. Once you do this, you can save the audience, but you can also sync the audience in nearly real time so that you do not have to upload again when your list grows.

Let's say you start off by uploading 5,000 people to your custom audience, but that you are getting a few hundred new leads a month as well. You can sync your CRM to Facebook using a tool like Driftrock so that as your database of leads grows, so does the Chunky Middle (and the Sweet Spot, below). Mailchimp and many other CRM/email marketing tools are also starting to make real-time Facebook Custom Audience syncing a frictionless process to set up.

You can also use the Facebook Ad Custom Audience feature to hide your ads from people. Maybe you do not want your competitors to see your ads or you do not want to show your ads to the segment of your email database that already bought from you. Just like you can add and sync a CSV file that will see your ads, you can add and sync a CSV file that will never see them.

3. The Sweet Spot.   This is your audience that has already become a lead in your database and is most likely to buy now. This audience should see all your C^3 ads: content, conversion, and closing.

Because they are already in your database as a lead and have thus shown intent in your product or service, you want to (and can appropriately) show them ads at the bottom of the funnel featuring customer reviews, scheduling a time to speak with sales, calling now to learn more, getting a discount by acting now, or signing up for your next group sales webinar.

Creating this audience is as simple as uploading every lead you have right now, and then syncing it (again, using Driftrock or a comparable tool) so that as soon as a new lead comes in, new closing ads are triggered for this "sweet spot" audience.

For example: One of my closing ads that performed well when targeting my sweet spot was "We're not stalking you, we just want to talk." It linked to a tool I use called ScheduleOnce (also known as MeetMe.so), which lets people book their preferred date and time for a one-on-one sales demo (while syncing with most online calendar programs, ensuring it doesn't conflict with my existing schedule). An ad this focused on closing might be a HUGE waste of money if I targeted it at the Magic Million or Chunky Middle, but because I am targeting only the leads in my database who have already shown intent in buying, it works.

Most people think that once they've got a lead, they don't have to market to them other than by email, SMS, or calling to follow up. That's so wrong. Your Sweet Spot audience should be seeing ads that keep them engaged with you until they buy. Remember, emails typically get opened by considerably less than half of the people who get them. Using this follow-up advertising technique, you can pay to get your closing campaigns in front of nearly 100 percent of your leads anytime you want!

When you set up your Facebook funnel properly, the lead doesn't FEEL like they're in a funnel at all. The progressions through it are very natural, and the types of content and calls to action they see get more aggressive only if and when they show more intent.

To review, here is a quick look at how the C^3 of Facebook ads and the three audiences you want to target are interrelated:

Content marketing ads target the Magic Million, Chunky Middle, and Sweet Spot
Conversion marketing ads target the Chunky Middle and Sweet Spot
Closing marketing ads target the Sweet Spot

Pro tip: There will be some times when a conversion ad makes sense to target the Magic Million or when a closing ad makes sense to target the Chunky Middle. Just know that while you can get more leads doing this, you will also pay for more clicks from people who don't register for your list or want to talk with sales yet. But if you ever need to "boost" your lead flow, just target the Magic Million with the conversion ads and target the Chunky Middle with the closing ads.

Another pro tip: Day parting provides an additional level of customization you can use for maximum lead conversions. Through day parting you can set your Facebook ads up to be displayed only at certain hours of the day and/or on certain days of the week. I've used this and it's very effective, especially if you want your ads to run while you have a salesperson on the clock who can follow up instantly. Also, knowing what time of day your ad will run allows you to get VERY clever with your copy and relevancy. Imagine an ad that runs on Friday and Saturday night only between the hours of 1 A.M. and 4 A.M. that starts with "Do you have trouble sleeping on the weekends?" or an ad that offers an amazing deal, but only on Tuesday afternoons. When you combine the three Cs with the three audiences and then add day parting, you can really set yourself up for better lead generation and better lead conversion.

Determining Your Facebook Ad Budget

You can run Facebook ads for as little as a dollar a day, but that doesn't mean you should. If you are serious about making Facebook ads a constant channel for acquisition, you need to have a decent, ongoing budget in place.

I find the best way to determine your specific budget would be to ask yourself, "What is a monthly budget that I can afford to lose that I can commit to for a year to see how this goes?" It's a lot like a trip to Vegas: Even though you might hit it big, you have to be okay with losing every single dollar. If you're in it needing the ROI immediately, you're going to end up quitting before the plan starts to click. Don't get me wrong, you can get clicks, leads, and sales today with Facebook ads. Just like you can burn calories and build muscle today by going to the gym. But you aren't going to actually get in shape without consistent commitment.

The difference in lead volume between a $1 to $2 a day budget and a $10 to $20 a day budget is quite literally 10 times. Winners are willing to lose before they win. They're willing to invest, lose, and learn. Thankfully, by using this chapter as a guide, you won't "lose" nearly as often as you win.

People always ask me what a good cost per click or a good cost per lead from Facebook is. My answer? Don't obsess over either of those metrics. Just make sure they're not WAY too high to get an ROI, once you know what your true cost per acquisition is (cost of leads required to close one). If it's $10 a click or $100 a lead, you better be selling something awesome AND expensive to make up for it. But having a low cost per click or cost per lead is not our endgame, either. Cost per acquisition is. Honestly, anything between $0.10 and $10 a click can be deemed "good." Cost per lead of $1 to $100 could be "good." You need to calculate what is good *for you*.

If you set up a campaign for a month, you shouldn't check how it is doing every hour. But you do want to keep an eye on how it is performing compared to par. If you launch four ads that you're going to run for 30 days, look at them each after five days. If one ad got you 1,000 clicks for 38 cents each, and one got you 200 clicks for $2.38 each, it would be foolish not to take the budget away from the low-performing one and throw the budget at the one that's already succeeding. By keeping an eye on their performance, you can double down on your ads that perform well and kill the ones that aren't working. You can also go to the top of your page, click "Insights," Posts, and then sort by which ones are getting the most clicks. Sometimes paying to reboost these ads is a smart play.

To judge the overall success of an ad campaign I make sure I have at least 100 leads from it. Not 100 clicks. 100 leads. Sometimes I will generate up to 200 leads before I judge a campaign. Why? Because I am focused on conversions, not leads. By getting 100+ leads from a campaign, I feel like I can better judge the quality compared to getting 10 "bad leads" and bailing.

The Facebook Relevance Score can also help you keep your ads on the right track to success. If you're getting good scores by Facebook's standards, the next ads you run will benefit out of the gate. If you are historically good at running ads, Facebook will automatically assume your next ad will be good, too. Achieving a high relevancy score (Facebook uses a simple 1 to 10 grading scale) comes back to the principles of great images, great copy, great CTAs, and great targeting.

Pro tip: Remember that the longer you try to run an ad, the less likely it's going to stay relevant. Things change. So keep an eye on what Facebook calls frequency (how many times the average person has seen your ad so far). If you see that an ad has been seen dozens of times by the same audience and is losing steam, change it. Alternately, don't give up on your ads after they have been seen only a few times by each person. Often, it can be the sixth, seventh, or tenth time someone sees your ad before they click.

FOUR FACEBOOK AD TYPES EVERYONE SHOULD RUN

Once you nail the content for your ads and determine your custom audiences, you will then need to determine what *type* of ad to run.

Facebook has a ton of ad types to choose from, none of which I would call bad. But there are certainly some ad types that work better than others. Here are four Facebook ad types that any business can and should be running.

Ad Type 1: Boosted Post

This is by far the easiest ad to set up. Post something to your page and then boost it for a day. If it does really well, you can always reboost it or even open it in Ads Manager and fine-tune it later. Boosted posts allow you to closely control your budget with short spurts of exposure. As opposed to a big, scary monthly, quarterly, or annual budget, you can make a dent with boosted posts in just one or two days without breaking the bank. Boosting a post is also the quickest path to quality engagement of your ad. Properly done boosted posts get a much higher relevance score than other ad types, in my experience.

Pro tip: Try uploading a photo album of pictures to your page with a link in the post to a landing page, and then boost that. When you upload an album, it actually creates a beautifully designed entry in the news-feed when compared to everything else that has only one picture. Plus, it gives you more chances for a click that catches their attention than only the link to your lead magnet. With an album, people can actually swipe through all the pictures and then click the link when they are ready. This works great for our real estate clients. They can include 10+ photos of a property by doing this in one ad! By showcasing more photos and descriptions, it can keep tire kickers from clicking though, thus increasing the conversion rates of your landing pages by sending fewer but better qualified clicks.

Ad Type 2: Click-to-Website

This one is pretty straightforward. You could think of it as your Facebook ad fastball down the middle. The purpose of this ad is simply to get as many clicks as possible, all going to one place.

Ad Type 3: Multiproduct/Carousel Ad

If you want to drive people to multiple parts of your site or multiple landing pages, you can use a multiproduct or "carousel" ad. This is one ad that simultaneously pushes people to multiple places using tiles that are swipe-able.

An example might be an ad that had multiple CTAs, like (1) Buy my book, (2) hire me to speak, (3) check out my fast-growing company, and (4) check out my Facebook group. In this one ad, I can now funnel people to Amazon, my landing pages, my website, and my Facebook group. I have found that these multiproduct ads, with their beautiful interface in the newsfeed and interactive design elements, can get the best cost per click and highest CTR of anything I have ever tried.

Pro tip: Try using multiproduct ads in super creative ways by using a panoramic shot or design elements that work together even though they are on different tiles. I ran an ad where we connected the tiles visually using plus signs and then an equals sign to end the ad, and it got rave reviews and results.

Ad Type 4: Lead Ads

Facebook has never shown a more obvious commitment to helping business owners get leads as they have with their new Lead Ads option. Lead Ads do not require you to link to a landing page or website to collect someone's information. They don't even require the visitor to fill anything out, as Facebook already (in most cases) has their email and phone number on file. Instead, when someone clicks on a Lead Ad, it instantly (and by instantly I mean MUCH faster than a normal landing page would load) pulls up a simple form that is pre-filled with their information so they can simply click Submit.

One of the primary reasons Facebook created this ad unit was for mobile. Waiting even a second or two for a page to load can feel a lot longer when we are on our phones. Another was that many small business owners have terrible websites and landing pages and were simply wasting their money driving traffic to them. If you are looking to get a huge list of emails and/or phone numbers that you can add to your database, Facebook Lead Ads are an excellent choice.

Facebook Power Editor

Power Editor is Facebook's more advanced interface for creating and maintaining ads. Power Editor allows you to do more advanced, agency-centric tasks (like tagging your ads for organization). If you want to mass edit an ad campaign, it's helpful. If you need a dashboard to see all the different campaigns you're running, it's helpful. You can even use Power Editor to mass upload ad campaigns via a CSV file to save time.

But for most people, Ads Manager and boosted posts provide more than enough options. Everything I have covered in this chapter so far (except Lead Ads) can be done without Power Editor. In fact, if something gets added to Power Editor that takes off and is genuinely useful to marketers (like multiproduct ads or day parting or Lead Ads), Facebook typically adds that feature to Ads Manager (or even to the boosted post ad options) quickly.

Pro tip: If you want to learn more about Power Editor and all of its advanced capabilities, I highly recommend checking out Jon Loomer's blog. He's become an authority on Power Editor and regularly provides detailed blog posts about changes, helpful tips for Power Editor users, and great advice about Facebook ads in general.

Once you have your Facebook funnel launched and then fine-tuned, you will have an endless supply of leads coming in each and every day.

In fact, now that we have locked down the New Internet and I taught you how to be a Facebook marketing expert, you can start getting "greedy" by looking at some of the other social networks and tools I use to get more traffic, leads, and sales.

Chapter 5

Simple Strategies (Beyond Facebook) That Drive Massive Traffic and Leads to Your Website and Landing Pages

Facebook may be greater than everything else when it comes to traffic, leads, and sales, but "everything else" can also be an untapped reservoir of tremendous growth. The key is to use a scalpel, not an axe. The best strategy is to go deep on a couple of repeatable tactics that work for you as opposed to going wide and throwing a ton of things against the wall to see if they stick. You can't crack The Conversion Code without a blueprint. And sure, the blueprint will evolve and change. But if you add more to your plate every time you read a new how-to blog post, watch a free webinar, or attend a technology conference, you're going to end up bloated. You can quickly become a jack of all Internet marketing skills and a master of none.

I've mentioned this before, but I think it is worth noting again before you dig into the nuggets ahead. If you skipped this entire chapter, you could still crack The Conversion Code by executing all the others.

For most businesses, it is impossible to be *great* everywhere. Sure, you may have accounts on Twitter, LinkedIn, Instagram, YouTube, and Pinterest. Maybe you even link to them from your website and email signature (if you need a new email signature, check out WiseStamp). You may even update them a few times a week. But what have those accounts given you back in return for that half-assed investment? Probably not much you could take to the bank and deposit with dignity.

This digital "race to the bottom" in an attempt to be everywhere and do everything can be as deadly to a business as any virus. The cure is critically thinking and laser focusing on the few things that matter most. And maybe even more importantly, it's choosing the tools you actually already like and use!

For me, video has been huge for making sales, and I enjoy it. One big advantage that I've experienced using videos as my primary lead magnets and in most of the marketing I do is that my leads can get to truly know me and my company better than they could through written text alone. Remember, words are only 7 percent of how humans communicate. When someone reads an article or blog post, they apply their expected tone and physiology to it as they read it, not yours (unless they happen to know you). On camera, all 100 percent of the ways we understand each other are in play.

This is exactly why my Curaytor cofounder Jimmy Mackin and I host a live web show (#WaterCooler) and produce countless webinars, plus put the audio-only version of everything we do on iTunes and Stitcher, all for free. It's because there's a big difference between people hearing about you and hearing from you. Video allows for zero ambiguity in my message.

Bottom line? You want to produce content that's best suited for YOU. For some people, that's writing a blog post. For some, it's recording a podcast for iTunes, Stitcher, or SoundCloud. For some, it will be photo blogging on Instagram and Pinterest.

As it is nearly impossible to do everything listed below (unless you are a huge company with tons of money and resources), choose wisely. An easy way to do this would be to think about what *you* like the most of what is listed below, regardless of potential lead volume, advertising opportunities, or clever hacks that sound enticing. Do you organically find yourself using LinkedIn a lot? Are you on Instagram all day? Do you *love* podcasts? Do you watch YouTube more than you watch television? If the answer is yes, you will have a competitive advantage out of the gate when you do start to advertise and do lead generation there. I have personally found the following tactics to have a solid return on the time and money I spend investing in them.

EMAIL MARKETING

I am going to go much deeper into email marketing best practices for lead follow-up and long-term lead nurture campaigns in Chapters 6 and 7. There really is no better way to get big traffic that consists of the people most likely to buy from you, on demand and for nearly no cost by the way, on your website than from a well-composed mass email. If you heard that email was dead, you need a new source. It may be more difficult than ever to break through the noise of a crowded inbox, but even average email open rates are still between 21 and 23 percent and average click-through rates are 2.7 to 3 percent (per Mailchimp).[1] This means that if you have an email list of 10,000 people, you could get 2,300 of them to open something and 300 of them to click a link to something anytime you want. Now imagine if you apply what you learn later in Section Two and got dramatically higher open and click-through rates, like I do. And what if you had a 100,000+ email list? The math gets very exciting.

Email marketing is a critical component of The Conversion Code. Most companies are doing it very poorly, if at all. Not only can a cleverly crafted mass email send massive traffic when and where you want it, but also the data you gather about who opened and clicked your messages will help you identify those "most likely to buy" from you.

I find that an alarming number of people, even the ones who do send mass emails, don't truly understand just how impactful they can be. Did you know that you can actually see your email marketing traffic in Google Analytics? If you use Google's easy-to-use URL Builder to track your links before you send your next campaign, you can better understand the impact your emails are actually having. Imagine having the additional insights around how long the people who clicked in the email stayed on your site, how many additional pages they looked at while they were there, and so forth.

I find time and time again that the website traffic generated from my email list creates some of the highest time on site and page views per visitor of any of my sources. I can't recommend enough reading Chapters 6 and 7 before you send your next mass or drip email.

RETARGETING

One of the reasons that I recommended installing tracking or retargeting/remarketing pixels in Chapter 1 is because they can provide one of your best sources of traffic and leads, plus they are great for "being everywhere" online while a prospect is looking for products and services you may offer.

Basically, retargeting is the act of presenting additional ads to someone who visited your website or landing pages. With the proper tracking pixels installed, you can "follow up" with these prospective leads without ever capturing their email address or phone number. With the ideas you learned in the last chapter about Facebook marketing and ads combined with the ideas you will learn in this chapter, retargeting is the glue that holds it all together.

Think of it this way: No matter what you do, most of your traffic will not opt in. But the fact that they even visited your site in the first place is a *great* indicator that they are serious about needing what you sell. Using AdRoll or the Facebook tracking pixel, once someone visits one of your pages, they will see more and different ads "following" them around. You have probably experienced this for yourself if you have visited Amazon or Zappos, only to start seeing their ads in your newsfeed immediately. A little creepy? Sure. Effective? Yes!

Setting up a retargeting campaign is actually pretty easy. And you won't have to update it often (we try to refresh ours quarterly). You are basically just building ads before you need them, knowing they will trigger over and over each day as people visit your website. Like with anything else you do online, image is everything. Make sure your ads really pop and stand out. The way you design an ad for a mobile banner is very different than the way you would build a Facebook ad.

Retargeter provides seven best practices for running retargeting campaigns:[2]

1. **Don't overbear or underbear**: Just because someone visits your website does not mean that you should overwhelm them with ads. You also don't want to show them too few ads. Retargeter "found that setting a frequency cap of 15 to 20 impressions to each of your users every month is the most elegant way to keep your brand top of mind."

2. **Make sure your ads are well branded**: The reality is that most banner ads don't get clicked on. So retargeting needs to do more for you than get clicks and leads; it needs to build your brand and get your customers telling you that "we saw you everywhere online." You want your ads to look great and have a strong CTA, but you can also brand them!

3. **Understand your view-through window**: Not all leads will click on your ad; some will actually see your ad and then type your URL into a new tab or window. So when that happens it should also be considered a conversion. Most retargeting software will give you this data.

4. **Have an incredible network**: Retargeting does not work very well if your audience size is tiny. Remember, these ads are conditioned upon people visiting your website or landing pages to trigger. If necessary, you can supplement your retargeting efforts by using the Google Display Network so you can reach *all* of your possible customers as they search the web, not just the ones you tagged who visited your site.

5. **Optimize your conversion funnel**: Your ads won't matter if where you send the clicks doesn't convert. Make sure you use all of the landing page design tips I covered in Chapter 1 when you deploy a retargeting ad.

6. **Target an actionable audience**: When you choose who to retarget, you do not have to choose 100 percent of your visitors. You can actually retarget based on the specific page they visited. Imagine retargeting only the people who had visited your reviews page—and retargeting them with more reviews. Or what about showing the people who got all the way to your contact page and then bailed some additional Contact Us CTAs? By getting micro with your retargeting, you can really have a macro impact on your conversions.

7. **Segment your active audience**: Not only can you retarget by audience, but also you can "burn" an audience when you retarget. This can be useful if someone actually buys and you don't want them to see more ads. By placing a burn pixel in your Thank You or Order Confirmation page, the ads will turn off automatically. You can also launch additional campaigns for this burned audience in the future. This can create solid upsell and retention opportunities when used properly.

CURATION

I am the cofounder of Curaytor, so I am guessing you may have seen this one coming! You may not always have the time or skill to create compelling original content or blog posts. But you are probably already sharing content that you found interesting or useful on other websites and blogs. Curation can help keep your audience engaged by finding and sharing great content from elsewhere. It can also help supplement the original content you create. But did you know that you can also use curated content to drive traffic and leads back to your site?

Snip.ly makes it very easy to "attach a call-to-action to every link you share." Even though you are sharing content from someone else's site, you can drive traffic back to yours using cleverly designed buttons and banners. Snip.ly is like a Hello Bar or Kissmetrics Engage tool, but instead of it being on your website, you can add it to any site!

Not only can you drive traffic like this, but also you can strategically place your brand on the most respected websites in the world, for free. The next time you share that insightful article from the *Wall Street Journal* or the *New York Times*, anyone who clicks it will also see your "ad" (see Figure 5.1). You can even add the Snip.ly plug-in to Chrome so you can do all of this with just one click.

Figure 5.1

Another great platform for curating (and benefiting from) other people's content is Genius.com. Originally a website where you could add annotations to rap songs (the original name of the site was actually Rap Genius), the site has evolved and recently become much more useful to marketers by allowing you to "add line-by-line annotations to any page on the Internet." Imagine reading a well-written summary of your industry's current trends and being able to highlight and add your two cents *before* you share it. By doing so, the additional insights you added will be highlighted and clickable in the text. Conveniently, you can also add links back to your website, social media profiles, or blog posts inside of the annotations you add.

YOUTUBE

If you are making videos for your business, but have not thought about them as a lead generation tool, think again. A great video can increase conversion rates on a landing page, better convey your message in a Facebook ad or press release (I use PRWeb), and even drive up your email open rates. YouTube can also be a major source of traffic to your website, landing pages, and lead magnets thanks to their massive scale and current standing as the world's #2 search engine.

Here is a quick hack you can do today to start making YouTube a referring source of traffic and leads for your business: Go into your YouTube analytics and sort your videos by the most viewed. Be sure to note the average length of a view on these particular videos. Next, you are going to add what YouTube calls a "card" to the videos at a time interval that is about 25 percent of the average view length. So if I knew the average view of a video was four minutes, I would add the card at approximately the one-minute mark. The idea here is that if you show them the YouTube card (which is really just a nice way to say pop-up ad with a link to anywhere you want) too soon, they won't click it. And if you wait too long, they may never see it. There is no exact science here. Just be sure that at a minimum you are showing the card within the average length of that video's view. Use the cards to link to your lead magnets that are most related to that video's content. So if I had a YouTube video about Facebook ads as an example, I would use a card that linked to a landing page where they could also download "27 Proven Facebook Ad Templates You Can Use Today."

What I'm teaching you can be done for all of your YouTube videos, but it really has the most impact when you use it on your most watched (or ones you expect will be). Think of the card as a native backup pop-up. You may already have a pop-up from SumoMe or Kissmetrics on your site; now you have a "pop-up" on your videos as well! Remember, in order to crack The Conversion Code, you have to be purposeful, not passive.

You can also use a more professional marketing video tool like Wistia, which allows for email capture built right into the video and can redirect to any URL you want when a video ends. Wistia also allows for greater customization options when you embed the video player and provides more detailed analytics than YouTube. We use Wistia for our sales videos so we can track what percentage of the video each individual lead watched. Thanks to Zapier.com, which connects services that are normally not integrated, I can even have the Wistia data sync to the lead's profile in my CRM.

YouTube ads are another largely untapped channel for generating significant traffic and leads. You can create YouTube ads and target them based on location, gender, age, video topic, and/or keywords. Just like with their cards, YouTube ads can link to a landing page with a lead magnet and capture form. You can link to other videos you have made in the ad, but I usually link to a landing page.

There are TrueView, In Stream, and In Display ad options to choose from. With TrueView, YouTube can guarantee that your ad will be seen before the video the person was going to watch begins. In Stream and In Display will place your ad among the suggested other videos while people search for and watch other YouTube videos. With many of the ideas in this chapter, there isn't quite enough scale to make a huge dent. But YouTube has tremendous scale, so you can actually drive a substantial number of clicks and leads if you get YouTube ads right.

When running a YouTube ad, I hope it would be obvious that it's important to use a great video! If your video sucks, it doesn't matter how great your landing page is because no one will ever see it. Most of the TrueView ads won't be shown for more than 15–30 seconds, so keep them short, sweet, and upbeat.

There is a phenomenon in Silicon Valley around startups making "explainer videos." These are usually under 90 seconds and feature a combination of animation, screenshots, and voice-over. GoAnimate actually makes creating one yourself almost as easy as using PowerPoint. The metric you want to focus on here is retention rate of the video.

If you have a budget, and you are going to heavily invest in YouTube as an ad platform, you can hire a plethora of companies that make these explainer videos for you. Just Google "explainer video companies" and be sure to watch a few of their demos before reaching out. I have found that each company has their own style that you can gather from their website examples before reaching out for a quote. Pricing for these can be $500 to $10,000 or more, depending on the scope and quality of the work.

My last piece of advice about YouTube is simple: Use their analytics to figure out which of your videos work and which ones don't. Our YouTube channel has more than 5.5 million minutes watched. At one point, we went nearly 20 straight weeks producing a live, one-hour show. But it was grueling and we knew we couldn't sustain the pace. Thankfully, when we took the time to really dig into our data, 10 percent of our shows were actually responsible for almost 90 percent of our video views. It was quite clear after checking our YouTube analytics that certain topics (like Facebook marketing or mobile apps) and having a notable guest on (like Gary Vaynerchuk or Gary Keller) led to exponentially more views and leads. Knowing that, it was certainly much easier to slow down on the frequency of shows, while still maintaining our best quality shows, traffic, and leads.

Pro tip: I highly recommend downloading the YouTube Creator Studio mobile app (this is different from the regular YouTube app for watching videos). They actually built a separate app for people who create a lot of videos and want to look at analytics and engagement numbers or reply to comments, on the go. I actually find the Creator Studio mobile app interface to be much easier to navigate and understand than the full desktop YouTube analytics.

TWITTER

On the free front, I find Twitter to be an invaluable tool for learning and keeping up with my craft. However, I find the only way to truly make Twitter an enjoyable experience for me is to use Twitter lists. In theory, everyone you followed on Twitter would be awesome. But you will quickly find that more Twitter users are annoying than are interesting. As opposed to hurting anyone's feelings by unfollowing them, I simply never look at my standard Twitter timeline (shh—don't tell the folks I'm following). In order for me to see a tweet, I have to also add the account manually to a private Twitter list I built entitled

"Gurus" (and believe me, I bet most of the people on that list do the exact same thing—this is a best practice employed by many other power Twitter users). I have spent countless hours adding the smartest people and companies in marketing, sales, and technology to my Twitter list. This saves me hours each week, because now all the best content is being filtered and brought to me. I no longer have to seek—I find.

I also add accounts to my list that I want to watch, but not follow. Let's say you want to keep an eye on what a competitor is sharing, without giving them the satisfaction that you "followed" them. Simple. Add them to your list—don't follow them. It is actually easy to make your Twitter lists private so that only you can see who is on them. For some context, here's the ratio of people I'm following versus who made my list. As I write this, I am following 3,720 accounts. My list has only 555 on it.

Another thing I keep an eye on is how often I am being listed by others on Twitter. Sure, it feels pretty cool to have 30,000+ followers (especially for a guy who was born in a city with only 47,000 people total). But I am tracking the number of times I have been listed more closely, even though it is a much lower number, at 1,300+. Check yours right now. How many times have you been listed?

One way to get listed (and thus looked at) more often is to keep an eye on your Twitter analytics. I don't spend a ton of time in them. But about once a month I will go into Hootsuite or Twitter to see what my top tweets were for Reach, Clicks, RTs, @ replies, and Likes. I also hop into Google Analytics to see the depth and length of the stays on my referring traffic from Twitter. Within minutes of looking at your top tweets each month, you will clearly identify what is "working" and what isn't. If you notice that tweets with hashtags, pictures, links, or YouTube videos happen to perform the best, do those more. If you see that no one ever engages with your tweets about beating a new level on Candy Crush, stop.

Pro tip: You can really geek out about your Twitter metrics and see who is the most engaged and the most influential from your connections. Commun.it, Sprout Social, and Klout all offer what I would call more "actionable insights" than Twitter's native Analytics tool does. Also, I use Tweetbot on my iPhone and Hootsuite on desktop, not the Twitter app or Twitter.com. I find the third-party Twitter apps are often superior to the native app.

Twitter's ads, like Facebook's and YouTube's, benefit from the scale of Twitter's user base and depth of their data-rich targeting options. You can target Twitter ads by location, hashtags, and accounts that follow you. But did you know that you can target them at those who follow other accounts in your field? Or accounts that might be followed by your ideal demographic? As an example, a local real estate agent in Las Vegas could target accounts hyperlocally, but could also cross-target that with criteria like that they ALSO follow HGTV, Zillow, or Louis Vuitton. Is your product the next great basketball shoe? Target your Twitter ads at users who already follow @Jumpman23, @FootLocker, and @Nike.

When creating your ad, you can choose between getting more followers and getting more engagement (clicks, RTs, replies, etc.) on your tweet. Right now, the cost to get a quality click is affordable. This is mostly because it is still too difficult to convert a Twitter click using a landing page due to most of their users being on phones. Twitter is working on creative solutions to this problem like Twitter Lead Generation Cards which are similar to the Facebook Lead Ad type I discussed in the last chapter (they better, as their stock certainly depends on their ability to drive leads to brands), but for now I recommend using a "light" landing page. Like I discussed in Chapter 1, by "light" I mean you ask for email or phone only. At this point, it remains rather difficult to get a lengthy form filled out after a click in Twitter.

Here is the nice thing about retargeting and having our Facebook tracking or AdRoll pixel installed on our website and all landing pages: The click is enough. I can drive thousands of clicks from Twitter to an article and couldn't care less about how many I capture while they are there because I know that just based on their visit, a Facebook newsfeed ad and a web retargeting campaign will be triggered. I am especially bullish on Facebook newsfeed retargeted ads. You can set up a retargeting campaign for someone who visits your blog so that the next time they log into Facebook, they could see an ad in their feed that says, "Thanks for checking out my blog. Here is a free download of X that you will probably enjoy, too." So you'll have cultivated the lead on Twitter and sent them to your site, and their site visit triggers an ad in their Facebook newsfeed and across the web as they browse that links to a landing page. Boom!

No matter which of the ideas in this chapter you end up using to get more traffic, remember that having a proven retargeting campaign behind it allows you to stress less about the immediate capture for times like this when it is tougher.

INSTAGRAM

Purposefully getting more followers on Instagram takes a few proven tactics. One obvious way is to take and share amazing pictures. Another one is to use popular and relevant hashtags. TagsforLikes .com actually makes finding, copying, and pasting the most popular Instagram hashtags, by keyword or topic, simple. Another way to get more followers on Instagram is to like several pictures in a row of the same account and then follow that account. This makes it impossible for them to miss your "chunk" of engagement when they check their notification stream among all their other one-off alerts.

I've also found images with quotes over them do exceptionally well on IG and can help increase your follower count and engagement level. Try using a simple free tool, like Pablo from Buffer, or a mobile app, like Over or Retype, to build professional-looking versions of these in seconds.

What I am most excited about with Instagram, however, is their ad platform. Most of my excitement comes from the fact that they are owned by Facebook, who has demonstrated that they believe quality ads and ROI are important. Combine that with the undeniable scale that Instagram has reached at this point, and the value of ads on the platform seems like a no-brainer.

One of the early knocks by marketers about Instagram was that you could not have a link in your posts or pics, only in your bio. Ads fix that. With Instagram ads, you can link to a landing page or to your website. Instagram ads are so integrated with Facebook that I even had to use Facebook's Power Editor to set up my first one. If you combine Instagram's addicted, daily users to Facebook's amazing data, you have a match made in Conversion Code heaven.

While it is too early to give you a well-vetted list of ads that work on Instagram, the best practices of a platform typically dictate what its best ad practices will be anyway. In my early tests of Instagram ads the cost per click, volume of clicks, conversion rate, time on site, and page views per visitor were all rock solid. How did I do so well having never run an Instagram ad before? If we know that awesome pictures, filters, hashtags, and text over images already work well through personal profiles and nonpaid business posts on IG, they should carry over to ad best practices, too. I simply ran Instagram ads that were in line with the already established ecosystem so they worked.

GUEST BLOGGING

A fairly new phenomenon has occurred in the past few years that is worth noting and taking advantage of. When I first started blogging, it was 100 percent up to me to get eyeballs on my content. This is the primary reason that so many blogs became ghost towns. It isn't exactly fun to spend hours researching and writing a great post, only to find that the only person who read and shared it was your mom.

Today, you can hop over to Medium or LinkedIn and publish a post that can be seen by their readers, not yours. The first time I published a post on Medium, it got over 17,000 views—99 percent of which came from their community, not mine. Of course, inside of the post I had several links back to my stuff, which got me some solid referring traffic. Here's the catch: I studied the Medium ecosystem and thought critically about what I should publish there. I knew my typical "how-to" articles would not go viral. So I wrote a very heartfelt piece about my wife and kids being away for the summer and how much harder that was than not having my phone for a day or two. The Medium community loved it and recommended it, and Medium featured it on their home page and a few other key places on the platform.

You should also identify any blogs or websites that are influential in your industry and send them some original content to publish. Inman News has been around for 20+ years in the real estate industry and reaches a C-level audience that I normally do not. So a few times a year, I will send some killer content to Inman that I know their readers will love and share. I find that when you send in a piece to just about any outlet or blogger and add "my last article got 17,000+ views and hundreds of social shares" or "I can also email it out to my 15,000+ email list," they don't ask too many questions.

When you do guest post, make sure that you have a strong author byline attached with links back to your best stuff. Also be sure to include a couple links in the article to other things you have written that are relevant to what they are reading but are housed back on your site. It's a very natural flow for someone who reads an awesome post by a new author to see who wrote it and dig deeper, maybe by checking them out on Twitter or visiting their site. Make sure you make this a requirement in exchange for giving them your killer free content.

PODCASTING

I'm addicted to podcasts. Podcast perfectly bridge the gap between text and video, creating a third channel, which includes new, untapped times to connect with prospects. People love our web show. But we can't expect them to watch it while driving, jogging, or showering. Having quality audio content, with well-placed lead magnets and offers, for these lengthy "downtimes" is quickly becoming a must. Podcasts don't bring back physiology like videos do, but not everyone is good on video and they do at least get you back tone.

In many ways, podcasts are the new blogs. Looking at the influencer marketing landscape, many (if not most) of the bloggers who gained a large following by writing have either moved onto podcasting or have added one (or more podcasts) to their arsenal.

If you are going to take podcasting seriously, pro tools are a must. If your podcast sounds poor, its results will follow. Once our web show

took off, we knew we needed to reinvest. Even though our show originally airs live on YouTube, it is largely a conversation that drives the
show's content. That is to say we don't use slides or screen shares—we
just use Google Hangouts, have a great guest on, and shoot the shit over
a beer about why they are so successful. Knowing that podcasts could
help us reach a new audience at new times (and because the show was
a moneymaker already in the video format), we went out and bought
Heil mics and Mackey mixers so that when we extracted the MP3 file,
it sounds just as good as if we had recorded it as an audio-only podcast
to begin with.

For some perspective on the results of publishing our content
across multiple platforms, now when we get 10,000 views on a
YouTube video, we get an additional 3,000+ downloads on iTunes
and Stitcher. I use Libsyn and Amazon Web Services for the hosting
and analytics. Even if you are not ready to become a pro podcaster
just yet, but you do want to dip your toe into the audio water, try
SoundCloud and your mobile phone. You can embed the results on
your site and share it or you can share it natively from SoundCloud
(which has a built-in community who can also discover it, much like
YouTube does for videos or Medium does for written content).

*Pro tip: Add bumpers to the beginning and the end of your podcast
with clear calls to action, like "Text this code to this number to get this
freebie" or "Go to our website dot com slash podcast to download the show
notes and a list of all the resources mentioned on the air." You don't just
want to get thousands of listens. You also want to get hundreds of leads.*

Even if you do not start a podcast, consider advertising on one.
I can literally name every sponsor of all my favorite podcasts and
have taken action on many of their various offers along the way. My
company even hired a lawyer through hearing about his services in a
podcast ad. My cofounder bought an engagement ring from a company he heard advertising locally on Pandora's ad network. There
is just something about repetition combined with auditory ads that
really make them stick. Sell things in Boston? I am sure there is a
HUGE podcast right now with a rabid Boston fan base, and I am also
sure they need some sponsors. If YouTube ads are the new lower-cost/
results-based television ads, then podcasts and Pandora ads are the
new lower-cost/results-based radio equivalent.

WEBINARS

I am sure you have attended a webinar in the last few years. But have
you actually used webinars as a lead generation and conversion tool
for yourself yet? If not, you are REALLY missing out. Webinars open

up two entirely new types of "sales pitches" for you: the group pitch and the 90 percent pitch-free pitch. Use them both to go beyond the "one-on-one" sales call option.

This opens up a huge new lead type: There are a large percentage of people who just do not want to put themselves in a position to be one-on-one with a salesperson. Period. There are also a large percentage of folks who just won't hear out a sales pitch of any type.

By having a "group demo" option, you can attract people who normally avoid the one-on-ones. And by having the "pitch-free pitch" (meaning you spend the first 90 percent of the webinar teaching and not selling, then quickly pitching, and closing with a solid one-time offer during the last 10 percent), you can attract exponentially more people when you market education versus marketing a sales pitch. In fact, let's say you get five times more attendance when marketing a webinar where you bring value than you do one where you pitch. At my company, we can get 5,000+ signed up for a takeaway-focused webinar we produce. In comparison, getting 500 attendees on a group sales demo would be solid. But the fact that you don't pitch the entire time does not mean you close at a 5x lesser rate than your one-on-one pitches. In fact, because you get so many more people tuned in when the content is great, the net results can actually be better.

Any time you do a big webinar, it can also be a huge day for traffic to your site and landing pages. I've found that having a few links ready to drop into the chat as I present and then mentioning them as I go can drive a tremendous amount of traffic and fresh opt-ins.

A well-presented webinar with a well-positioned one-time offer can net you a higher closing rate than you might imagine. Even though what we sell at Curaytor costs more than $1,000 per month, I consistently close 10 percent or more of our group webinar attendees. I make the offer and show a number to call (I use BetterVoice.com to track the number of calls and to route the leads and any missed calls to our CRM). They call in to get the one-time offer. My sales team uses the script in Section Three of this book to close them at the highest rate possible. Plus, the added bonus is that you grow your email list much more quickly when A/B tested against sales pitch-only marketing.

Don't think about your sales options as only one-on-one calls and one-on-one demos, all primarily focused on your product or service. And don't forget that the people attending these webinars are often people you would have *never* closed before, because without webinars you weren't even giving them an option they would bite on. Once the webinar ends put the recording on YouTube and then embed it into a new post on your blog. Don't forget that Webinar recordings also make for great email marketing, Facebook ad, and landing page content.

Pro tip: If you do start producing webinars, you want to get a minimum of 50 percent who register to also attend. Some call this "show rate." Make sure you send out supplemental reminder emails. Don't just rely on the webinar tool you use to follow up. Also, not everyone will call in or email in, but I have found a small hack that gets me even more "I am ready to buy" chances from my webinars—when you make your offer at the end, tell anyone who wants to buy to put their cell phone number in the chat box and you will call them ASAP. It is a beautiful thing to see those numbers come flying into the GoToWebinar chat box. The second you close out the webinar, run an attendee report and start dialing. All the numbers they put in the chat box will be in a CSV file!

Growth Hacking

I actually hate that term, but growth hacking is a tactic that can pay off in a big way when done properly. Growth hacking can actually mean a million different things. Here is how I think about it and use it to get more leads and make more sales.

Who do you know who has a huge email list or social media presence that does not overlap with yours all that much, but consists of people who might buy from you? If you provide enough value and have strong relationships in place, "using" someone else's audience to grow yours can have a big impact. I placed "using" in quotes because I do not mean that you literally get their email list or that they get yours. You just work on creative campaigns together that can be promoted to both.

I used to work for a company called Move Inc. Through a deal they have with the National Association of Realtors to operate Realtor.com using their brand, they get access to virtually every email address of every real estate agent in the United States (well over 1,000,000) and they are allowed to market to that list (as long as they follow agreed-upon guidelines). My audience is tech-savvy, top-producing early adopters. Their audience is every agent with a pulse. So when we team up to do a webinar together, they get me thousands of leads that I could not have gotten otherwise and I get their brand in front of my modest but sought-after audience. We've successfully collaborated several times, frequently getting more than 5,000 people to register. Four thousand of those came from their list, not mine.

Influencer Marketing

When I first started using Twitter I was definitely "doing it wrong." All I did was connect some app that would push my Facebook page updates over to Twitter as tweets. Then I set up a few spammy tweets that repeated each week and never really logged back in. It came as no surprise the first time I checked my analytics to see how my tweets were doing (they almost all had links back to my site in them) that they weren't even making a dent.

So I took a step back and looked at Twitter as a place to meet, follow, and connect with the brightest minds in my industry. It turns out I wasn't alone—most of them didn't know how to use Twitter the right way, either. So I learned along the way, and what I picked up on was that while you could certainly share your links, it was proper etiquette to share others' more frequently. So I started tweeting and mentioning people I looked up to and started retweeting their best tweets as well. Within no time, they started to return the favor! Within 30 days of changing my strategy, my traffic from Twitter more than tripled. Even though I had tweeted a fraction of the amount of times I had before, because now the traffic was coming from THEM, not me.

The same ideology applies to any influencer outreach you may do. As Gary Vaynerchuk would frame it, you have to jab, jab, jab before you right hook. I once had Robert Scoble and Mari Smith share the same link to my blog with an interview I did with a friend who had a Facebook page with 47,000+ fans (that is what they were called at the time) taken away without warning. Within moments, there were 6,000+ people on my site at the same time! Remember, I had just recently passed 3,000 page views in one day. Now I had 6,000 uniques all at once.

When it comes to trying to get influencers to help you spread your content, it would probably be more like jab, jab, jab, jab, jab, jab, jab, right cross. I was at least on Mari's radar. Mari was on Robert's radar. How? Write about them. Write about what they write about. Share their stuff. Send them emails. But be realistic, too. You can kiss an influencer's ass from all the right angles, but if you do not have A+ content for them to share, you are dreaming if you think they will share something average. They became influential by being excellent, not average. Be the same.

As I mentioned to open this chapter, "everything else" (besides Facebook) can be an untapped reservoir of tremendous growth. It is also entirely possible to experience tremendous growth without anything but Facebook as your main focus. If you do decide to move beyond Facebook, I hope executing on these specific ideas I've provided helps you as much as they have helped me. As the choices of where one can market online continue to increase, make sure you are social networking with a plan and purpose instead of social not-working.

In Section One you've learned how to crack The Conversion Code on capturing more leads. But the fortune is in the follow-up! Now it is time to start creating quality appointments and closed sales from all these Internet leads. Section Two will give you the blueprint for turning new and old leads into appointments. Then in Section Three I will teach you exactly what to say on the phone to an Internet lead so that they say "yes."

Part

II

Create Quality Appointments

Chapter 6

How to Use CRM, SMS, and Marketing Automation to Immediately Turn a New Lead into a Hot Appointment

Internet lead generation (and most of what I taught you in Section One) is relatively new. Because so many companies are still trying to crack the lead generation code that you just learned, they don't even realize that there is a much more difficult and important code to crack next: the lead conversion code.

The following data (*source*: Move Inc.) from the real estate vertical around the increase in volume of online leads between 2011–2014 sums up perfectly what is happening for every industry. There are MORE leads than ever before to be had, but finding the needles in this new massive haystack will require a plan.

In 2011, there were 2.9 million real estate leads generated online and 4.4 million home sales. By 2014 the number of leads skyrocketed to 40.6 million, while home sales had only increased to 5.1 million.

The entire purpose of this section is to help you clearly and quickly identify the best leads to call and use the script you will soon learn in Section Three on.

Marketing feeds appointments. Appointments feed sales. Sales feed our children.

LEADS VS SALES - 2011

2.9M : 4.4M

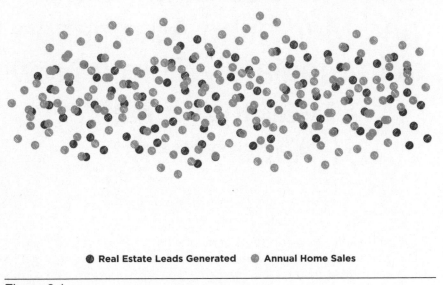

● **Real Estate Leads Generated**   ● **Annual Home Sales**

Figure 6.1

THE FORTUNE IS IN THE FOLLOW-UP

Now that you have leads regularly coming in, the real work starts: Ensuring you create quality sales appointments on a consistent on-demand basis. In Section Two, I will teach you how to turn hot, new, and old "bad" Internet leads into appointments and show you how I use automation plus a person (scheduler) to turn new leads into instant appointments for my sales team (closers). Technology will be a huge part of this, but having the right people in place matters even more.

You need to decide before you proceed what boat you are in regarding resources. In a perfect world, you have someone dedicated to calling every new lead as quickly as humanly possible in an effort to schedule them quickly for a lengthier call with your "real" sales team. As soon as they say they want to speak further and they are interested, only then is the actual salesperson looped in. You can "hot transfer" the lead on the spot or book them for the near future. In the next section, I introduce a 20/20/20 sale. If you have what is sometimes

LEADS VS SALES - 2014

40.6M : 5.1M

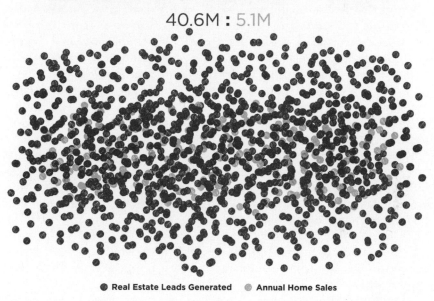

● **Real Estate Leads Generated**   ● **Annual Home Sales**

Figure 6.2

called an ISA (inside sales associate) on your team, they will basically be doing the equivalent of the first 20: gaining control, digging deep, qualifying, and uncovering objections, before transferring to a closer. Another way to use an ISA is to leverage them to call your old leads so that your higher-commissioned salespeople don't have to get told no as often. When a salesperson can focus on selling while a scheduler focuses on appointments, you create a much better quality of life for everyone.

Far too often talented salespeople get a job thinking that their leads and appointments would be handled for them and all they had to do was pitch, only to later learn that that they also have to spend much of their time cold-calling and prospecting to leads who would *never* buy right now, but might be willing to set up a semiserious call if you catch them at the right time, with the right script. Salespeople should be selling not scheduling.

If you are the scheduler and the salesperson, it gets tougher but it is not impossible. In fact, when we started Curaytor, I was the marketer, the scheduler, and the closer! I am guessing I am not the only one who has had to wear more than one hat. And even though it was tough and I started losing my sanity, I got us to a couple of million dollars in annual recurring revenue without any additional employees in marketing or sales. For additional insights into using this bridge role and the upside of not making your highest-paid commissioned salespeople call leads and instead spend most of their time on pitching, check out Aaron Ross's great book *Predictable Revenue*, where he shares how he grew the inside sales team at Salesforce.com to a $100 million a year channel using this same methodology.

If you are only going to be selling, not marketing or scheduling, feel free to jump ahead to Section Three right now. But if you need a blueprint for turning new and old Internet leads into quality appointments for you or your sales team, stay here and read on....

Leads are meaningless if someone does not work them and follow up with them in a systemized, strategic, and repeatable way. It amazes me that people are willing to spend a small fortune on leads, but then don't hedge their bets and spend nearly as much time, money, and resources on converting them.

If a takeaway from Section One was that demand generation is greater than demand fulfillment, think of what you will learn in Section Two as appointment generation being greater than lead generation.

Appointments get us one step closer to our real goal, closing sales (Section Three).

SPEED + TENACITY + SCRIPT = HIGHEST CONVERSION RATE POSSIBLE

Because Internet lead generation and conversion are so new, the *best* advice about lead conversion is typically built around speed to respond (see Figure 6.3).

And on being tenacious in the number of follow attempts you make (see Figure 6.4).

Bottom line? *Speed* and *tenacity* (plus using the script in Section Three), what I call STS selling, is the only way to crack The Conversion Code.

Just remember this quote (and never forget it) from Gaspar Noe's *Irreversible* when you think about lead follow-up: "Time destroys *all* things." Your ability to convert an Internet lead will be directly impacted by your ability to contact them *fast*.

In fact, you have a 100x better chance of turning a lead into a conversion in the first five minutes than you do after just 30 minutes. Plus, you can increase the percentage of leads you contact from 48 percent to 93 percent by calling six times, not once. Don't call once the

Figure 6.3   Impact of Speed-to-Response on Lead Conversion

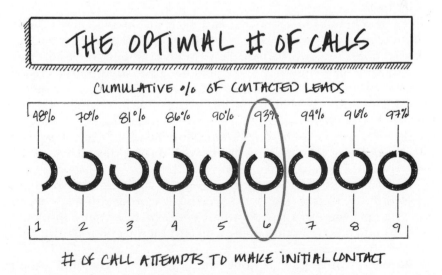

Figure 6.4   The Optimal Number of Calls

BEST DAYS + TIMES TO CONTACT LEADS

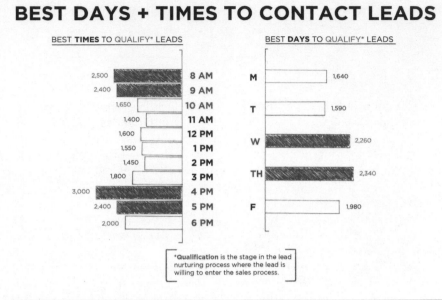

BEST **TIMES** TO QUALIFY* LEADS

2,500	8 AM
2,400	9 AM
1,650	10 AM
1,400	11 AM
1,600	12 PM
1,550	1 PM
1,450	2 PM
1,800	3 PM
3,000	4 PM
2,400	5 PM
2,000	6 PM

BEST **DAYS** TO QUALIFY* LEADS

M	1,640
T	1,590
W	2,260
TH	2,340
F	1,980

*Qualification is the stage in the lead nurturing process where the lead is willing to enter the sales process.

Figure 6.5   Best Days and Times to Contact Leads

first day and again on day two. Call on minute 1, minute 10, minute 30, hour three, and day two, as an example. Meanwhile, the median time for a company that does call back is three-plus hours and 47 percent of companies *never* even respond, yet we always blame the leads for being "bad."

It's also helpful to know that calling leads during certain hours and on certain days works best (see Figure 6.5). The ideal time to call leads in order to convert them is between 8 and 10 A.M. and 4 and 6 P.M. Calling on Wednesday and Thursday gives you the best chance at reaching someone. This makes perfect sense. You can get someone on the phone BEFORE their day gets going or as it is winding down. You also have a much better chance of contacting someone during the middle of the week than you do on a Monday or a Friday. Basically, when people are driving to or from work during the middle of the week is when you have the best shot!

But let's be honest: Ideally, someone on your team is calling all day, every day. For those of you who simply cannot call leads all the time, be sure you use a scalpel when you schedule your call blocks. Sadly, I know a LOT of salespeople who NEVER start their day by 8 A.M. and are off the clock by 4 . . .

Beyond calling quickly and often, which you should set up reminders for in the form of an action plan applied to all new leads in any CRM, you must also use automated emails and text messages to complement your quick calls in order to achieve the highest conversion rate possible.

SMS > EMAIL

When I get a new lead through one of our landing pages that collects a phone number, I use an auto SMS with merge codes that says, "Hi [lead first name]. I got your information from [lead source name]. Can you talk now?" We often get more *replies* to that text than we do *opens* of our first drip email. Why? Speed matters, so does personalization, plus our inboxes are clogged when compared to our SMS messages.

We use a CRM called Follow Up Boss that sends the text message for us (and also sends our drip emails), but there are other tools out there, like Twilio, BetterVoice, or SendHub, that have some neat auto SMS (as well as mass SMS) features.

Another way we use SMS to create appointments from our hot leads is by putting a dozen or two of them on one list and bulk texting them (if you send to less than 25 at a time in SendHub it doesn't make you include the "REPLY STOP TO OPT OUT" disclaimer), asking if they have time for a call today. "Hey [first name]. It's Chris from Curaytor. Can you chat?" is about all it takes to get a flood of responses when you do this, as long as you focus it on hot leads who have been opening and clicking emails or visiting your website most recently.

Using auto and bulk SMS messages to convert new and hot leads is one of the biggest untapped opportunities in lead conversion today.

EMAILS THAT WORK

The fact that you call and text doesn't mean that you shouldn't also send automated email messages to your new leads as they come in. The first message is especially critical as it will get the most opens of any that you send. I can't believe how many companies waste this critical opportunity by sending something like, "Thanks for your inquiry. We will be in touch." Am I actually supposed to be impressed by or reply to that?

Instead, craft initial drip emails that are more human, ask for a reply, and sound less canned, like, "I just got your information from Zillow. Is now a good time for you to speak?" or "I appreciate you filling out that form on our website. I know it can sometimes be scary to do that. Is now a good time for you to speak?"

Don't think of your new lead drip emails as converters—think of them as conversation starters. They'll ultimately lead to conversions more quickly anyways because conversations are what create closes. Not drip emails.

Beyond the first message, come up with several more that you sequence and space out strategically. When I get a new lead, I send them an automated email on days one and two, and then again on days four and seven. That is four follow-up emails in the first week compared to most companies who never even follow up once. And because the emails I send are so simple and human, humans often respond to them. Imagine that. There is no better feeling than getting a lead AND a reply from them to your first automated email. Sadly, there is no perfect sequence or spacing, but keep in mind that every day and week that passes will lower your open and click-through rates with a lead.

In fact, because email open rates drop off so dramatically over time, you will learn in the next chapter that I actually do not send any drips or automated emails to leads after the six-month mark. Everything from that point on is freshly crafted and real-time.

Another solid message to add throughout your new lead campaigns (or to send to all of your old leads all at once) is the "just checking in" email. This one crushes it for us:

Subject line: Checking in
Body: I was just checking in to see if you needed anything from me today.

That's it. I'm not kidding. I have spent hours and hours on longer, more well-written emails that tried to impress leads. They never do better than this bite-sized, conversation-starting approach.

Pro tip: If you do have names or other data for your leads, make sure you use merge codes. You can even put merge codes in subject lines and SMS messages so that even though they are automated, they feel personal. As an example, if a real estate agent got a home value request that included an address, they could merge that field into their reply so that it read, "Subject: Home Value for [address]," or even if you have just a first name you can send things like "Chris, check out these new listings." The data shows us that using this personalization can cause dramatic increases in opens, clicks, and replies.

By "bursting" your calls, texts, and emails closely together, you will contact leads at the highest rate possible. Think of the phone, email, and text as a team, not individual players. The nice thing is you can automate both the email and the text message. If you are going to call, you should also text them if they don't pick up. Or after you send an email, text them to let them know it is in their inbox. Or as you will learn in the next chapter, after sending mass emails, pick up the phone and call the ones who were most engaged with it.

In a perfect world, you could call every lead that came in right away. They would pick up. You would close them. But we live in a far from perfect world. So focus on speed, tenacity, and using multiple channels of follow-up (plus the script you will learn in Section Three when they do answer the phone) to ensure that you are converting the highest percentage of Internet leads you possibly can.

Need More Appointments? How to Use Email Marketing, Retargeting, and User Tracking to Turn Old Leads into Quality Appointments

Everyone thinks the cure to their online ailment is more leads. That if somehow you just continue to add leads to the top of your funnel, the middle (appointments) and bottom (sales) will work themselves out somehow. Good luck with that. You need as much purpose and strategy, if not more so, to turn an Internet lead into an appointment as you do capturing them in the first place.

Here's the good news. Old leads buy things, too. I promise. In fact, I can take just about any email list (like the one you probably already have or the one you now know how to grow quickly after reading Section One) and get a few appointments and sales immediately. It isn't their fault you didn't convert them yet. It's yours. After you read what is in this chapter, there will be no excuses left for letting hundreds or thousands of leads die a slow death when there is a proven way to resuscitate them.

Don't trip over nickels (leads you already have) just to pick up pennies (more new leads). If you already have old Internet leads (including at least their email address) who never responded to your past attempts (or lack thereof), you can create appointments en masse with smart mass emails. In fact, I'm about to share an email that you can send today to all of your old leads at once that will almost certainly (and instantly) resurrect some for you and turn them into quality appointments.

But you have to make a deal with me first. You have to promise you will not use any type of HTML email template when you send this email. The design should just be a plain old email like you would send to a friend or colleague, using Gmail or your phone. I don't mind if you use some type of email signature that looks nice. You just cannot use a highly stylized template for this email, period.

Better yet, if you want to crack The Conversion Code, you have to commit to not sending mass emails to people that look like an ad the second they open them. This design-less email ideology even applies to your automated drip emails (covered in the previous chapter) that you will be sending to new leads as they come in.

Remember the study that taught us people have eight-second attention spans? Well, it takes me only one second to look at an email in my inbox and mentally dismiss it as an "ad," ensuring I would NEVER reply, simply due to the formatting. How about you?

I am not against having some well-thought-out nice images or links or even a nice email signature with your logo in it when you send a mass email. But I am against gaudy email templates that look like the latest Target ad, repelling conversations much more successfully than they start them. Conversations create clients. And no one wants to have a conversation with your ugly-ass monthly email newsletter.

You might think that after spending so much time in Chapter 1 on the importance of design, I am a hypocrite for not just suggesting here that you build a beautifully designed email template to use. I'm not. In Chapter 1, I was talking about building trust with the strangers who were visiting your website. Now I am talking about building trust with the people you have captured and are already on your email list. Emails are not best used as mini billboards for your website. There is a better way. . . .

So with that being said, here is the email that you can send today to all your old Internet leads in an effort to create some appointments. I would really appreciate it if you would email me (Chris@Curaytor.com) if this works for you.

Subject line: Quick question
Body: Are you still looking to buy [INSERT WHAT YOU SELL HERE]?
Signed,
You

That is the entire email. I'm not kidding. I hope you weren't waiting for anything groundbreaking or Shakespearean. This will work better than what you have been sending for a million reasons. But it works mostly because it doesn't waste the lead's time and it gives them a huge out if they want it. We tend to write more when we don't know what to say. Most people write their emails according to the famous passage, "I have only made this letter longer because I have not had the time to make it shorter," written by Blaise Pascal in 1657 (and often misattributed to Mark Twain).

Literally, the only thing you can change before you send it is the [INSERT WHAT YOU SELL HERE] to what you sell and the word "buy," but only if it makes more sense to write "sign up for" or "hire" based on your business model. If it were I sending it, I would write, "Are you still looking to sign up for Curaytor?" If I was a mortgage banker selling loans, it would say, "Are you still looking to refinance?" If I owned a catering company, it would say, "Are you still looking for a caterer?"

Another top-performing cold lead email we send in a similar vein simply has the subject line "Checking in" with a body consisting of "I wanted to check in and see if you needed anything from me today."

But, seriously, you must resist the temptation to add more. I know it is hard. I know you want to turn the corner and be all like, "Are you still looking to sign up for Curaytor? Our clients love us, our software is amazing, and Inc. just featured us. We would love to speak with you about helping you grow your business through Facebook ads, email marketing, and marketing automation ..." Don't.

This less-is-more approach, in an effort to convert leads, may have actually been invented in 2009 by a marketer named Dean Jackson, who talked about a "nine-word email." Dean recommended a subject line that uses the lead's first name, like "Hey, Lisa" or even just their first name as the subject line, like "Bob." If you send this email one at a time, adding the name is a no-brainer.

Sadly, though, I find that even the people who do have a big email list still do not always have names for all of them. If you do have a list with name and email, you can use a merge code for the first name in the subject line to accomplish the "Hey, Lisa" personalization at scale.

I am sure you are already worrying about the fact that you will also hear a lot of "No" in reply to this email. Don't let this bother you. Find pleasure in this. Plus, sending people follow-up emails when they admittedly no longer want them or are point-blank telling you they are not going to buy just doesn't make any sense. If people do not want to buy what you sell and are willing to take the time to reply and tell you so, that is an ambulance you shouldn't chase anyway.

If I burn a few old leads with this approach, but I get dozens of "Yes, I am. I'm glad you reached out!" replies from a bunch of

Internet leads I thought were dead to begin with, that is a trade-off I am willing to make. Especially knowing that getting more leads is very easy.

THERE IS NO LONGER AN OLD LEAD BUCKET

Beyond this one-time jolt to your list that you can also repeat semiregularly as old leads pile up, you should treat the content you send through email to your old leads each month like gold, if you want it to become currency. I have a "no drip" policy when it comes to leads that are older than six months, when the initial marketing automation campaigns I covered in Chapter 6 have run their course. Instead of prewriting canned emails months or even years in advance and putting your leads on a long-term email campaign, commit to spending a minimum of a few hours each month researching, writing, and sending "real-time" emails.

I even have a simple method you can use for finding ideas for "fresher" emails to send each month. I use Buzzsumo.com to do some research by keyword, source, or topic, which will show me the most socially shared articles online that match my query. As an example, one month we were researching an email that we draft for our real estate customers to send to their databases. Through BuzzSumo I found that an article about "she sheds" was at the top when I searched "real estate." The article had been shared millions of times on Facebook even though I was unfamiliar with the term. The massive social shares also made me feel good about using the source. I was guessing that if we got an email out quickly we would be the first to bring "she shed" (the female equivalent of a man cave) into people's consciousness, causing a reaction in the form of replies to our clients who we sent the email for. I was right. The email was a huge hit. Our clients got a ton of responses (many of which started with "I want a she shed! By the way, we need to sell our house. Let's talk."). We also very soon thereafter started seeing segments about she sheds on the national news and being covered in mainstream media.

You don't have to send boring, vanilla messages about what you sell just because you are marketing to leads. By finding topics and tidbits that are relevant and related to what you sell, not just transferring your sales pitch into an email campaign, you can craft follow-up emails people actually read and look forward to. Your open rate, click-through rate, unsubscribe rate, and reply rate will all thank you!

Each time I research, compose, and send my mass emails, I make sure they fall into one (or more) of these three simple buckets:

1. **Educational:** Will the recipient learn something useful and want to thank me by replying?
2. **Entertaining:** Will the recipient smile and want to thank me by replying?
3. **Conversational:** Will the recipient want to continue the conversation I start by replying?

As I have said before and I will say again, conversations create customers. I often look through the past email campaigns that companies have been sending before they hire me. The most common mistake I see is a lack of question marks at the end of the messages. Although many of the leads you send emails to will not reply no matter what you send, without asking specific questions to close out your messages you aren't even giving yourself or them a fair chance. You don't have to be spammy. Just make it conversational. In the example of the she sheds email, we simply asked to close out the email, "I think I actually want one of these! Do you?" We knew that *guys* would not be able to resist answering if they wanted a she shed. And we were pretty sure the ladies on the lists would more or less reply, "Hell, yes, I want one!" Our instincts were right on both counts. But without the question mark, the volume of replies would have been a fraction of what it was, regardless of the email's quality. This is the same ideology we applied to our new lead follow-up emails as well. Clever. Question.

Another great way to find content for your emails is your blog. If you are regularly creating content, mass emailing the best of it to your list with links back to your posts (or videos/podcasts) can allow you to increase the frequency at which you send. I am often asked how often is too often to send emails. The answer really lies in quality. If you publish an amazing, insightful new post, you should want as many people as possible to read it. If an article is average, be willing to be self-aware about that and not email it out. Just like you wouldn't write an email about everything you found in BuzzSumo, only the best and most shared. Treat your own content the same way. Just never forget that your email list can be some of your first, and most frequent, readers.

Pro tip: While you do not want to schedule emails months in advance, you should set reminders for yourself in your calendar right now so that you do not forget your "email marketing" or "lead follow-up call" days. We all start with the best intentions. You are probably going to want to execute a couple of these ideas I've given you immediately. But will you execute week in and week out, or at least month in and month out, long term, without a nudge? One nice thing is that when you send emails like the ones I am suggesting, they work, which makes time blocking doing them much more fun to do.

Now that you have a quick blast email template and a long-term email strategy under your belt for your old Internet leads, I want to share with you two things that I am confident you are not doing yet, that when combined with the email ideas I just detailed will take your lead conversion rate to new heights.

Pick Up the Damn Phone

Simply sending out emails with no additional phone calls to follow up is not going to help you crack The Conversion Code. Here's the good news, no matter if you use MailChimp, AWeber, Constant Contact, or any of the other countless mass email marketing tools they all provide at least the basics you will need of who opened and who clicked in your emails.

Let's say you send out your clever little monthly or weekly blast email on a Tuesday at 2 P.M. local time. You should have the rest of Tuesday and the first half of Wednesday blocked off to call every single lead who opens and use the script you will learn soon in Section Three. Now, if you have a ton of leads and there are hundreds or even thousands of people opening your emails, making it impossible to call them all, then switch your sights to the leads who opened AND clicked.

As I mentioned before, the average email click-through rates are often under 5 percent. So that means for every 1,000 leads you send to, only 50 are clicking—a very manageable number. Even if you had 5,000 leads, it would be only 250 people to call, which a good inside salesperson could do in two to three days. Also, the larger the list, the larger the list of people who open and/or click your emails more than once! Be sure to sort your list by those who opened your email or clicked it the most times. I am always amazed at how many people open an email 2, 5, or even 10+ times. When they do, I pounce.

You will be amazed at how much easier it is to call old Internet leads when you know that they were recently engaged. And how much better and confident your conversations can be when you have that insight as a salesperson. Think of these as "hand-raiser" leads, begging for you to call them and answer their questions about what you sell.

The best salespeople treat an old Internet lead with the same enthusiasm they treat a new one, given a good enough reason to. I couldn't care less if I got a lead in my funnel 14 or 4 months ago. If

I sent them an email with the subject line "Save $500 on Curaytor" or "Facebook Tips for Top Producing Real Estate Agents" and they opened it a few minutes ago, I'm calling their ass.

User Tracking

Another way to use a lead's behavior to identify whether it is worth calling them is to install user tracking software on your site and/or landing pages. Tools like Woopra, Mixpanel, and Intercom can help you identify who from your database is visiting your website, exactly which pages they looked at, and how long they stayed. Plus, you and the lead can both get real-time alerts based on a formula you predefine.

This means that not only could you call who opened or clicked in your emails. You could call those who clicked but then also stayed for more than five minutes and while they were there read your About page and testimonials. I am so bullish on user tracking as a lead conversion and sales tool that we have it built into our platform at Curaytor and are constantly trying to make it more useful. It is music to my ears when I call a lead and they start by saying, "I am actually on your website right now (or watching your demo video). But I am guessing you already knew that. Wow, you guys are good!"

You can also trigger messages, like little trapdoors on your site, so that when a lead comes back to your site and does X they get email Y because of it. Their behavior (or lack thereof) on your site can determine which email messages they get. As an example, you could set up a trigger in Mixpanel that if someone on your website visits your Testimonials page, it emails them a few more, immediately. Or if they watch a recorded webinar it emails them an invite to the next live one. The possibilities truly are endless. Just grab a pen and paper. Think critically about this and write out the triggers and the messages you want happening. Then get that loaded into a user tracking software so it can work over and over again as leads stumble into your "traps."

Have you ever been on Amazon, not actually bought anything, and then conveniently moments later an email from Amazon with a product you checked out appears in your inbox? They are doing exactly what I just taught you.

Technology has moved beyond simply reminding us to call because a week has passed or every lead getting the exact same message at the exact same time by email. You have to move beyond time- and date-based follow-up and start thinking about behavior-based follow-up.

With user tracking that triggers messages to be sent, your website becomes like its own little choose-your-own-adventure game for each lead. If someone is using the crap out of my site, there is a good chance that they would want more emails from me, too. Or better yet a call! The opposite is true as well. If someone has not used my site in months, it might be time to trigger a "nine-word email."

ADS AS A LEAD FOLLOW-UP TOOL

As I covered in the chapter on Facebook, retargeting your database of leads with ads containing content, conversion, and closing marketing messages brings a new and impactful way to stay in front of Internet leads, beyond email, SMS, and phone calls. I cannot believe how many companies think that once they have a lead their ad campaigns "worked." The fact that a lead is in your CRM doesn't mean that you should stop showing them ads. In fact, because you know you have already captured their email and they are in your database, you can get pretty creative with the ads you use.

Don't be afraid to make a lead opt in again for a new offer. Through your mass emails and your retargeting ads, in addition to driving them back to your site, you should also send some of them back to landing pages where registration is again required. I have leads in my database who bought from me after they opted in a dozen or more times to various offers before the one that "worked" worked. This is why it is so important to treat old Internet leads with the same black Lab enthusiasm more typically reserved by salespeople only for a new lead.

Pro tip: If you have user tracking alerting you to call a lead who returns to your website, by clicking on retargeted Facebook ads (or your ads across the web) or in a drip, mass, or triggered email, you can really start to see your efforts working in conversion code harmony. If they click you call. If they return visit you call.

Everything I have covered in Sections One and Two has been leading up to this moment. So far, I taught you how to capture Internet leads and create quality appointments. Now, it's time for me to teach you exactly what to say to an Internet lead over the phone so that you close them at the highest rate possible.

Part

III

Close More Sales

Need to Know Exactly What to Say to a Lead on the Phone?

How to Have a Perfect First Minute on a Sales Call with an Internet Lead

Every *sale* is won or lost before it's ever *pitched*.

It is your job to immediately take control of every call(er). In this chapter, I will teach you exactly what to say during the first minute of your call(s). There are two *very* specific things (gaining control and ARPing) that you *must* do at the beginning of every call if you want to close the sale at the end.

Also, it is important to note that The Conversion Code does *not* involve cold-calling. Cold-calling is so 1980s. We are well into the twenty-first century, and during the past decade people have *willingly* put most of their life's happenings online. If you are in sales, social media should make you salivate. The ability to hyperpersonalize a sales call gives you an unfair advantage. These are Internet leads who you are calling and who at some point (ideally recently) willingly submitted their information and wanted to be contacted. Before you call, I will show you how to properly (and legally) stalk an Internet lead, and then use the intel you gather against them during the first minute of (and throughout) your call.

By the way, when salespeople (myself included) hear a term like "big data" or "social selling" we usually tune out immediately (and

P:60 = GC + ARP

puke in our mouth a little). That sounds too much like C-suite jargon. So instead, I simply think of it as using "big data" to make big bucks. Salespeople like money, not data. But what I do know as a fact and why I personally use the following techniques to stalk all my leads, pre-pitch is when I *hyperpersonalize* my sales pitches, I close more deals and make more money. Period.

So anytime I mention data, it is only as an enabler of me making more money on the phone. Ahead you will learn exactly how I quickly use social media (mostly Facebook), mobile apps, and Google searches to win the sale, before it even starts.

Thanks to the Internet and social media, it is easier than ever to "stalk" your sales prospects, gaining valuable insights that will easier enable you to close them at the highest rate possible. Gathering intel pre-pitch takes only a few seconds, is a repeatable process, and, most importantly, will impress the hell out of your leads, helping you close more sales.

Don't think about what you will learn in this chapter as "big data"—think about it as ammunition for your sales pitch. A bullet, with your lead's name on it!

THE TWO-STEP PRECALL LEAD "STALK"

Let's say you have a sales call scheduled with me and you are hoping I will buy your product or service. My name is Chris Smith. Seriously, that is my real name. In fact, it might be one of the most common first name/last name combinations in U.S. history. So, if you can learn how to gather intel on me, you can gather it on anyone. One thing to note here is that what leads provide on your various landing pages and website contact forms may vary greatly. At Quicken Loans, we had their name, phone number, email, address, current interest rate, current home value, and current loan amount. This data was not always accurate, but it was critical for us to have in order to make a call immediately and still have some solid, personalized talking points.

As I covered in the intro, it is *critical* that you are set up to call leads as soon as they come in. When that is the case, you will not have time to stalk. It is more important to make contact quickly than it is to gather more intel before you dial—thus the importance of collecting more information up front on the landing page.

At Fashion Rock, we had name, email, phone number, and what they hoped to become famous for. At Curaytor, we collect name, phone number, primary zip code, # of homes sold per year, and average sales price. Even though it's common knowledge that you'll get fewer leads when you request more info on your forms, each of the companies I've been a part of collected more than just name, phone, and email. It's not an accident, and this many successful companies probably aren't wrong. Why get that extra info when we know it will hurt our lead conversion rate? Because when our sales teams call, they have some SOLID talking points without doing any manual stalking whatsoever.

Note: What I detail ahead is most ideal if you have an appointment on your calendar at a set date and time with an Internet lead. When that is the case, I do what is ahead during the five minutes leading up to the time I am supposed to call them. Again, speed matters more than intel, so never stalk at the sake of speed to respond.

The entire purpose of your landing pages and the "stalk" I outline ahead is to gather two to four very specific data points (or items of interest) about the lead to use during your conversation. Our goal is to have a *strong, custom opening* to our script, like:

"Hey, **Susie**, my name is Chris Smith and I work for Quicken Loans. I was calling to follow up about your property at **123 Main St.** Looks like you currently have a **6 percent** interest rate and a loan amount of plus or minus **$400,000**."

OR

"Hey, **Susie**, my name is Chris and I work for Curaytor. I was calling to follow up about our availability in **90210**. I see here that you sold **150** homes last year at an average sales price of $500,000. That is awesome—congrats!"

OR

"Hey, **Susie**, my name is Chris and I work for Fashion Rock. I see here that you are looking to become a **model** and are in **Charlotte, North Carolina.**"

OR

"Hey, **Susie**, my name is Chris and I work for RE/MAX. I was calling about the home you found using **Zillow** over on **Madison St.** that is for sale and currently asking **$525,000**."

"Hey, _____, my name is _____ and I'm with _____. I was calling about _____ and I noticed _____, _____, and _____ before I called you."

In each of these examples, the bolded words are the unique data point and would have been available to me the second the lead came in. This is why a script is *so* critical. When you are trying to call an Internet lead within one second of them opting in *and* you want to sound competent, you need a plug-and-play approach like this.

When you do have more time to prepare for a pitch, you can do a much more advanced variation of what I just explained. Here is exactly what I do *before* every sales pitch that is at a set time and date:

Step 1 of the Two-Step Lead Stalk. I always start with a Google search. However, I do not just search for the lead's name (unless it is very unique). In my case, there are 3,730,000 exact matches for "Chris Smith" when you Google it. None of the guys pictured in Figure 8.1 are me, although I did always hope to play in the NBA one day.

Instead, you are going to Google search the lead's email address. By searching Chris@Curaytor.com, instead of "Chris Smith," the results are reduced to 13,900 total (and now they are all about me in some capacity). You can see Google found my company website (with phone number), plus my Facebook and LinkedIn profiles (see Figure 8.2); both have a plethora of information about my career, interests, and family life.

Think of a lead's email address as their online thumbprint or Social Security number. There may be millions of people with my name, but there are zero people with my exact email address. You should also use email addresses when searching for people on social

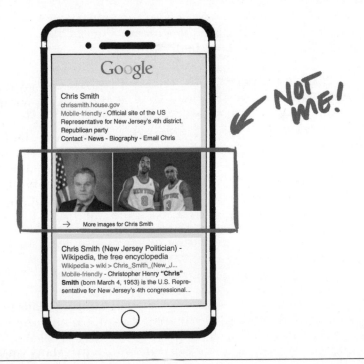

Figure 8.1

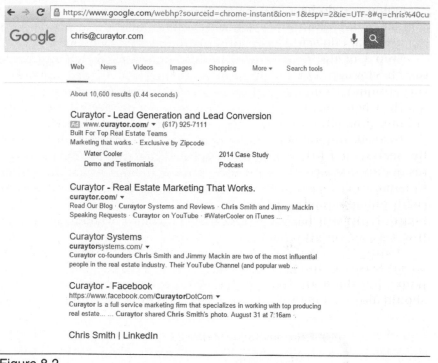

Figure 8.2

media sites like Facebook, Twitter, and LinkedIn. We all registered for those sites using our email address, so when you search by email it finds *one* result, not tens of thousands.

You should also do a quick Facebook search using their email address and/or phone number. When you find a lead on Facebook, it immediately opens up a treasure chest of personal information about them that is highly empowering for me as a salesperson. Because this is inside sales, finding a lead on Facebook also helps me remember that it is still a *person* on the other end of the call. I even find it helps to look at their profile pic while I chat with them.

Professional Sales Stalking Tools

There are also some pro tools you can use to stalk your leads prepitch when a Google search is not enough or does not return the insights you need. Spokeo, Intelius, Wink, Zabasearch, and PeekYou all also provide "big data" that is super useful for salespeople. Many CRMs also enrich the lead's profile automatically with "big data."

My favorite tool for stalking leads these days is an app called Charlie. Once you install it, it syncs with your calendar and provides an email alert or a mobile push notification to a data rich "brief."

Because Charlie syncs with my calendar I automatically get a one-pager about the lead 10 minutes before each of my sales calls are scheduled. Charlie will show you the person's interests and hobbies (the ones they grabbed for me are spot on: coffee, basketball, *House of Cards*, entrepreneurship), recent social updates, and Twitter connections in common. These "data points" become your "talking points" during the first minute of your call—perfect icebreakers for emotionally connecting with your prospect about something other than what you want to sell them and getting them to take their guard down.

Step 2 of the Two-Step Lead Stalk. Based on what you found in step 1, jot down two to four talking points or insights that prove you did your homework (leads always appreciate this). So in my case, you could have started your call by saying:

"Hey, Chris, it's Mr. Sales Guy from Company X. I saw a tweet you sent out yesterday about your Facebook groups and how Zillow actually made a change based on their influence. Impressive stuff! I actually spent a few minutes in the group you created, and it looks like you have built a special community. Congrats! The reason I called is that I saw you were interested at one point in what we sell and I wanted to talk more about it with you."

This strategy works even better when the lead happens to be a blogger or has been featured recently by the press or on a website in some capacity. The more specific what you find is, the more specific your opening can be:

"Hey, Chris, I just read an article about how you got your company Curaytor to over $3,000,0000 in annual recurring revenue in less than two years, and it really inspired me. I also sell technology for company X and saw you inquired at one point about our services."

OR

"Hey, Chris, I was reading an article you and your company Curaytor were featured in on Inc.com. Nice work!"

It is virtually impossible to say no to someone who does their homework and flatters you out of the gate, even in a sales pitch. No matter what level of success someone has achieved, we all like being told we are pretty before you try to kiss us.

The first widget of "the script" should include the following.

Your Four Custom Bullets

1. _____   2. _____   3. _____

  4. _____

"Hey, _____, my name is _____ and I work for
_____. I was calling to follow up about 1. _____.
Looks like you said 2._____, 3._____, and 4._____.
How are you today?"

These "bullets" will disarm the lead, let them know you are a professional, and make it crystal clear that *they* gave *you* their information. This is "unguessable" stuff and immediately separates you from the other cold callers.

Most salespeople start their calls like this:

"Hi, my name is Chris Smith and I am calling from Curaytor. How are you?"

OR

"Hi, my name is Chris Smith and I am calling from Curaytor. Is now a good time to chat?"

By inserting hyperpersonalized data points into our script at the *very* beginning, before we let them speak and before we ask our first "how are you?" or "is now a good time?" or "did I catch you at a bad time?" question, the person on the other end is much more inclined to hear you out.

That being said, this is still an Internet lead, not a referral from a friend or happy customer, so *we* need to have *our* guard up from the outset. After you have nailed your opening, next you need to gain psychological control over the caller. We need to begin the conditioning process (albeit subconsciously) so that at the end of the call, when we say, "Jump" (Buy!), they will say, "How high?" (*Yes!*)

How to Gain Control over the Call(er) with One Simple Sentence

So you just said something like this to start your call:

"Hey, Susie, my name is Chris and I work for RE/MAX. I was calling about the home you found using Zillow over on Madison St. that is currently asking $525,000. How are you today?"

What you say next is *critical*, and it needs to be the same every single time. Once you find a "gain control" statement that works for you, trust me, you should just use the same one every time. Here is exactly what I say next:

"I need you to please grab a pen and paper so that I can give you some information that isn't available online. Let me know when you are ready."

OR

"Can you please grab a pen and paper—I want to give you my personal contact information in case we get disconnected?"

OR

"I have some information that you are going to want to jot down. Can you please grab a pen and paper and let me know when you are ready?"

Then once they are ready I say, *"Great. My cell phone number is 555-5555 and my email address is* Chris@Curaytor.com.*"*

Notice the common element? By giving them an order to do something physical, and them doing it, it makes me/you the alpha. Will some people pretend to grab a pen and paper or be driving and unable to? Sure. But the people who will actually buy something will be willing to grab the pen and paper 95 percent of the time. If they are genuinely driving, just say, "No problem—I will email it over to you after our call" and move on to the next step.

A professional salesperson controls the call at every turn, none of which are more important than the opening of the call/relationship with the lead. Remember that tone matters a TON on the phone, so be very nice, but also be assertive when you ask them to do this. Think of it this way: If they won't grab a pen and paper to write a few things down, will they give you their credit card 20 minutes later? This technique of gaining control not only empowers you over those who will buy, but also helps to identify the more serious leads within seconds of the call starting.

After they write down the information you give them, the next sentence is pretty simple: "Tell me the primary reason why you inquired about _____."

The challenge is that everyone says some variation of "No" immediately. Leads/people are conditioned to put up a brick wall. Especially when a salesperson calls us. Our *job* in sales is to knock the brick wall down so that they will have a normal, human conversation with us. What I have learned is that no matter what you sell, during the first minute of a call with an Internet lead they will say something like the following:

At Quicken they would always say, "I just want to know what the interest rates are."

At Fashion Rock they would always say, "I just want to learn more about how it works."

At Curaytor they always say, "I just want to know how much it costs and if it is available in my area."

What they are all really saying is, "I don't want to be *sold*—I just wanted to learn more *before* I might buy."

The nice thing is that it is usually very easy to identify the "brick wall statements" that your leads will make day in and day out. Once you know them, the last step in a perfect first minute of a sales call

ARP

is to use a technique called ARPing. ARP stands for Acknowledge, Respond, Pivot.

Here is how you would acknowledge in each of these cases:

"I just want to know what the rates are."

Acknowledge: "You just want to know what the rates are. No problem!"

"I just want to learn more about how it works."

Acknowledge: "You just want to learn more about how it works. No problem!"

"I just want to know how much it costs and if it is available in my area."

Acknowledge: "You just want to know how much we charge and if we are available in your area. No problem!"

The acknowledgment lets them know with 100 percent certainty that you heard them. Remember, physiology is the number one way that humans communicate, and we don't have that luxury over the phone. Where normally as someone would ask you a question you would look at them and nod along so they knew you were listening and understood, on the phone the acknowledgment is the equivalent of the head nod. It also buys you a moment to think about what you will say next—the "Response." Thankfully, your responses will almost always be the same because you will identify responses that are comfortable for *you* to say and that work.

Here is how you would respond in each of the foregoing cases:

"I just want to know what the rates are."

Acknowledge: "You just want to know what the rates are. No problem!"

Respond: "The rates are currently at historic lows, and most of the people I speak with are saving a ton of money."

"I just want to learn more about how it works."

Acknowledge: "You just want to learn more about how it works. No problem!"

Respond: "The way the event works is that we put you in front of the best talent scouts in the world."

"I just want to know how much it costs and if it is available in my area."

Acknowledge: "You just want to know how much we charge and if we are available. No problem!"

Respond: "I will cover pricing once I feel like we can truly help you."

As you can see, with each response I am keeping it *very* simple and straightforward, but I am also never really answering their question too specifically. Remember: I am in charge, not them. We talk about what I want to talk about when I want to talk about it, or I *lose* and they *win*.

If your responses were "The rate is 6 percent," or "We charge $1,275/month," you will find that it will be a very quick call.

The last step is to pivot the conversation to where you want it:

"I just want to know what the rates were."

Acknowledge: "You just want to know what the rates were. No problem!"

Respond: "The rates are currently at historic lows, and most of the people I speak with are saving a ton of money."

Pivot: "How long have you owned your home?"

Acknowledge: "You just want to learn more about how it works. No problem!"

Respond: "The way the event works is that we put you in front of the best talent scouts in the world."

Pivot: "Have you done any acting/modeling/singing yet at the local level?"

"I just want to know how much it costs and if it is available in my area."

Acknowledge: "You just want to know how much we charge and if we are available. No problem!"

Respond: "I will cover pricing once I feel like we can truly help you."

Pivot: "How long have you been a real estate agent?"

The pivot gets the conversation back to where we want it.

It also leads us into the next part of the code: how to build rapport with an Internet lead by asking the right questions. The pivot question is the first in a series of questions that we will ask the lead in an effort to "dig deep," build serious rapport, and close them more easily.

The Digging Deep Technique

Questions to Ask That Make It Impossible for an Internet Lead to Say No

Did you know that 35 to 50 percent of Internet leads choose the first person they talk to?[1] That stat is sure to get salespeople and companies excited about being faster to respond and executing what I covered in Section Two. You don't even have to be the best as long as you are the first!

But what if you were first *and* best?

The inside sales mecca is quality leads + instant speed to response + increasing talk time by using a proven framework for your conversation on the phone. Remember: Gaining control and ARPing typically both happen in just the first 60 seconds.

Having what I refer to as a "meaningful conversation" is the key to conversion. Across the ventures I have been involved with and the range of products, services, and price points I have sold, I would estimate the average length of the calls where I closed a sale was 40 minutes. At Quicken, a perfect call for me was between 20 and 25 minutes. At Fashion Rock, it was between 30 and 40 minutes. At Curaytor, it is between 45 and 60 minutes.

Being able to identify these windows of time that typically pass before you can close and get paid matters. Going into a sales call knowing that "if this doesn't go 20+ minutes, I don't make a sale" will change the way you approach every call.

This was something I learned a long time ago while working at Quicken Loans. Quicken was so advanced with their technology in the mid-00s that some guy would wake up in the morning, he'd go to Yahoo.com with a goal of reading the financial news, he'd see an ad to get today's mortgage rates, he'd click, put in a little info, then a little more, and then Quicken (or one of their lead providers like LowerMyBills.com) would capture him.

I'd be on the phone with him less than 30 seconds later. People were equal parts impressed and freaked out.

What Quicken knew was that people didn't want to talk to multiple mortgage bankers (salespeople) if they didn't have to. It was then that I realized how easy the magical formula was: Be first and talk to them the longest. Do you really think people want to talk to two mortgage bankers or two realtors or two vacation salesmen? They don't even want to talk to one!

We'd also get some of our leads from Lending Tree. The whole point of Lending Tree is that five or six people are going to be calling you to compete for your business. Well, if I know Wells Fargo and Bank of America and everybody else is getting the same lead as me, I have to respond quickly and I have to have a long talk time. Because while I may not always have the lowest interest rate or closing costs, do you *really* want to go through a 30- to 45-minute loan application, have me pull your credit, and then hang up just to start the whole process over again with another sales guy? Probably not. Especially if I build rapport with you by digging deep!

So, yes, you have to be first, but you also have to be the best at increasing talk time and having meaningful conversations. If you're not ARPing and just give them the rate they were looking for, they're probably hanging up in two minutes and answering a call from the next company. If you can master the first 60 seconds and then start digging deep, you can take the 35 to 50 percent success rate of people just going with you because you were first up to 80 to 90 percent going with you because you were first *and* you were great. Closing this gap can lead to immediate, exponential growth.

THE DIGGING DEEP TECHNIQUE

Talk time is best increased and most valuable when used to DIG DEEP with your leads. When I do sales coaching, salespeople who are struggling always say the same thing, "Chris, I just can't close. How do I close? Will you listen to how I'm closing?"

You have to realize and be self-aware that you already won or lost the sale well before you "closed." If you can't close, it's probably because you can't dig deep. It's probably because you weren't gaining control of the conversation and using a proven framework and script that work every time.

DDT

Please write this down and put it where you can see it clearly as you call your leads each day. **"Dig deep or go to sleep."** That was in my cubicle every single day when I was making my sales calls for Quicken. Because I knew if I didn't dig deep and build rapport with this person, they weren't going to do a loan with me.

You want to script about four to six qualifying questions that you can use on every call. But the money is made by asking the questions that aren't scripted—the "digging deep" questions. Most of the scripted questions you will use are really just qualifying questions and conversation starters. While the best qualifying questions are specific to what you sell, there are certainly some "stock" questions that any salesperson or company can use to get started:

How long have you been researching _____?
Have you ever purchased anything like _____ before?
Why is now the right time for you to consider buying _____?
How did you hear about _____?

For a real estate agent, the scripted questions might be:

What is the number one reason you are moving right now?
How many homes have you sold before?
Have you ever worked with a real estate agent before?
What was the one thing your last agent did that bothered you the most?
What is your ideal time frame for selling your home?

As they answer each one, act like a four-year-old and simply ask more questions. Dig deep(er).

"How long have you been researching _____?"
"Wow! You have been researching for six months. That is a long time. What websites have you been using the most to do your homework? Oh, you like website X the most. Have you tried any mobile apps as well?"
"Have you ever purchased anything like _____ before?"
"You have? Nice. Did you have a good experience? No? What would be one thing they could have done better?"
"Why is now the right time for you to consider buying _____?"
"Oh, you and your wife are expecting your first child! Is it a boy or a girl?" "Is this your first child?"
"How did you hear about _____ _____?"

"You Googled us? Nice! That happens a lot. What did you think of our website? You liked it? Sweet! Is it important that you work with a 'tech-savvy' company?"

If you're not asking digging deep questions, you cannot close at the end of the call. You really want to hone in on their emotional and logical reasons for buying.

In fact, you want to literally write down their answers to the questions you ask, both scripted and unscripted. We are going to use their responses later in our call to make it virtually impossible for them to say no when we close them (their answers will be used during the Five Yes Technique in Chapter 12).

Digging deep seems like something that salespeople would do naturally, but they don't. I would shadow calls at Quicken Loans, and the lead would get on the phone and they'd say, "Hi, I want to get a home equity line of credit for $50,000." And the banker on the phone would say, "Great! I can help you with that. What are you going to use the money for?" (That's their version of digging deep.) The lead would reply, "Oh, we want to build a deck on the back of our house." And the banker would say, "Great! I can help you with that. Who is your current loan with?"

They were an order taker, not a salesperson.

Here is what digging deep really looks like, using the exact same example: "You're building a $50,000 deck? *Wow*. Tell me about it! Is this thing gonna have two levels and elevators in it? Why in the heck are you spending $50,000 on a deck, is it platinum? Does it cook the food for you when you have BBQs?"

The best salespeople are listening, taking notes, and have a genuine interest in their prospect's situation; they are not just waiting for the other person to stop talking.

If you don't listen, you can't dig deep. If you can't dig deep, you can't close. I've personally just always genuinely been interested in people. And why they make the choices they make.

So with my approach, they come back and say, "Oh, no, Chris, it won't have an elevator or be platinum, we actually have a lot of people over all the time and we love to have birthday parties at our house. We're at the point where my husband got a raise at work so we can finally afford to build the dream deck we've wanted for so long."

How different is that?! Now there's some rapport! Now I have some ammunition that is meaningful when we get further into the call and I *close* her. By digging deep, I am identifying the emotional reason for why they want to buy.

And at the end of the call I will make them say no to those emotional reasons for buying, not to me. That's a much harder pitch to say no to.

You have to dig deep so that when you go to close, you have the ammo for the Five Yeses. I'll get to that technique in-depth on page 127, but the idea is we would be recapping the answers to their digging deep questions to start our sales pitch:

> So you want a line of credit because you're building a deck, right? Yes.
> You're gonna have family over a lot, right? Yes.
> Your husband got a raise, right? Yes.
> You love to do barbecues, right? Yes.

You won't know what to say to start your close at the end of your calls if you don't dig deep at the beginning. Successfully digging deep means you can already start thinking about how it's going to help you close later.

Ninety percent of your competition is going to pitch their brand and product during the first part of their call. You instead will focus the first part of the call on *them* to crack The Conversion Code. Be prepared to ask specific qualifying questions and *listen*. If you're not willing to *care* and *ask why* and then ask why again you will never be an elite closer.

Once you realize there's rapport and you've dug deep enough, the next step is to build trust in your company.

Chapter 10

How to Build Trust with an Internet Lead in Two Simple Steps

Now that we gained control over the caller, ARP'd around any early brick wall statements, and dug deep so we truly know why they are buying, it is time for us to build trust.

Building trust requires more than simply building rapport while you dig deep. It is one level of success over the phone to get someone to like and trust you; it is another to get them to *buy* from you. Especially when others may also be vying for their business simultaneously.

When it comes to building trust with Internet leads, I find that keeping it simple and focused works best. In fact, I have identified only two things you need to say in order to build trust and move on to the next part of the call.

The two steps that most quickly build trust with an Internet lead are:

1. **Cobranding:** Who can you align your brand with that consumers already trust?
2. **Statistic:** How can you convey numerically that you are the clear choice to work with?

In the real world I have used this approach time and time again with success. Here are a few examples of how I have seen cobranding + powerful stat inserted into a sales script:

At Curaytor, we manage several million dollars per year in Facebook ads (cobrand) and our average client makes $500,000 per year (stat).

At Fashion Rock, our founder discovered Britney Spears, *NSync, and the Backstreet Boys (cobrand), so more than 65,000 people apply to attend (stat) our event each year.

1 + 1 = Trust

At Quicken Loans, our founder also owns the Cleveland Cavaliers (cobrand) and we are the largest online lender in the United States (stat).

As you may have noticed, these cobrand plays and stats are simple and to the point. That is why they work. In most sales scripts and when I listen to salespeople try to "build trust," inevitably they try so hard they end up sounding like a scam.

Remember, at this point in the call you have gained control, ARP'd, and dug deep. The digging deep section is especially important as the transition to building trust. You *just* listened to them intently, so in some ways they owe you one. While you have their earned attention for a moment, don't lose it. Keep it short, sweet, and to the point while building trust with an Internet lead so you can continue through the call frictionlessly.

Chapter 11

Proactively Uncovering Objections

One of the worst feelings in sales is getting to the end of an amazing pitch, fully expecting the person to buy, and then getting blindsided by an objection that you didn't foresee like, "Thanks so much for your time Chris, but I need to think about it." In The Conversion Code, the time to get objections is NOT when you are closing. It's actually before you ever even begin your pitch. Most salespeople focus on and practice overcoming objections; I focus on eliminating them. Early.

A very common "objection" in sales is that the person wants to wait and think about it. There are other common objections too, like the spousal—"I need to talk to my spouse before moving forward"—or the cost objection—"I want to buy, but I can't afford it right now." Heck, I have even heard "I need to pray about it" as an objection. The nice thing is at any company, these objections will start to define themselves (you probably already know what they are for you).

Expert salespeople proactively uncover these objections well before they ever get them. As opposed to being told that someone can't afford or commit to what you sell at the end of a 30 or 45-minute call, we're going to ask people if there is any reason they can't move forward today, now. In fact, there is no better time to absorb the blow of possible objections than directly following when you've built rapport by digging deep and established trust. Think of it as a quick window where you got them to let their guard down.

The following statement is all that you need to say to proactively uncover objections (if there are going to be any): "If we are able to accomplish your goals and you agree everything makes sense, is there any reason that you wouldn't be able to move forward today?" (if you sell something pricey with a longer sale cycle just say "this week," "this month," or "this quarter" instead of "today").

PUO

Typically, someone who is going to buy from you is going to have a very simple answer: "No."

If we accomplish their goals and everything makes sense, why wouldn't they be ready to move forward?

You will also find that this question will bring the objections out, so you can discuss them now, not later (when you're trying to close). If they say, "Yes. I never make a decision without talking to my wife first." Now that I know that, I can at least address that!

I can ask if we can get the wife on the call, too. I can ask if they're typically on the same page when it comes to things like this by asking, "If we did call your wife, and told her you were doing X, do you think she'd be on board?" or even when applicable, "We do have a 30-day money back offer, so just in case she's not on board, you can still address that without getting in the dog house."

As for the cost objection, you'd much rather them jump to the price now than complain about the price later. "Well, how much is it? I can't move forward today if I cannot afford it." If they ask that, don't get discouraged. This is a buying question! They're visualizing themselves buying and using your product or service. In the "real world" (outside sales), you'd be foolish to give the price before you pitched. If you were speaking in front of a crowd and someone stood up to ask, "How much is this?!" you wouldn't answer that question. You'd side step it and continue, letting them know that you will get to the price at the end.

But this is an Internet lead that is a click away from blowing us off at all times, and we haven't even pitched yet, so you don't want to give them exactly how much it costs, but you do want to give them a ballpark idea. If they are insistent on knowing the price early, you can still sidestep the question by saying, "Our packages start around X," or "Our monthly packages are typically between this and this. Is that way out of your budget?"

In some ways, this is the first close. You should get as excited about them saying "no, I don't have any objections about moving forward" at this midway point in the call as you do about them saying "yes, I want to buy what you sell" at the end of a call.

Again, in most cases, if you've done everything up until now correctly, you will find more people than not are willing to sweep their objections under the rug and tell you they won't bring them up later. That is *very* empowering to hear as a salesperson.

Now, when you get to the real close later, this is a human who has told another human that if it makes sense, they'll pull the trigger. It's very difficult for them to go back on literally saying, "No, if everything makes sense, nothing should stop us from moving forward."

Think of objections as people robbing you of the money you know you deserve to make. Or think about it another way: You've got to disarm the alarm (uncover objections), before you go inside the house (close) if you don't want to wake up the "No" monster.

Just like with building trust, proactively uncovering objections is not meant to be a long part of the conversation. You will already know by this point in the call if what you're going to pitch makes sense for them. "If we are able to accomplish your goals and you agree everything makes sense, is there any reason that you wouldn't be able to move forward today?" is a question that I call built for sales. You are taking advantage of the rapport and trust you have built thus far to get a quick "I promise not to give you an objection at the end" from the lead.

With any possible objections out of the way I have some very exciting news for you. Enough about them. It's (finally) time to start OUR sales pitch!

Chapter 12

How to Start Closing an Internet Lead Using the "Five Yes Technique"

Once you uncover any possible objections (or lack thereof), there is one last step before you start you pitch. It is called the "Five Yes Technique."

Before I share with you how to do the Five Yes Technique, I need to point out one critical thing that you must decide before you can proceed: Are you going to do a one-call or a two-call close?

If it is a one-call close, you would roll into the Five Yes Technique after you uncover objections and before you start your pitch, using Feature, Benefit, Tie Down (covered in the next chapter).

But I want to plead my case right now that most of you should use a two-call close. In fact, two-call closes are probably the right choice for most salespeople. I have developed what I call the 20/20/20 sale that makes using a two-call close make a ton of sense and easy to do.

THE 20/20/20 SALE

The first 20 minutes is everything up until now. You would end your call after Chapter 11, and you would tell them that you are going to call them back in 20 minutes to go over your proposal, product, or service, because you want to spend some time customizing your presentation based on what they just told you.

A good reason for breaking your call down into two calls is that it can be difficult (no matter how sharp your sales skills may be) to get and keep someone excited enough to buy for 30 to 40 straight minutes. By building them up during the first 20 minutes, and then spending the next 20 customizing and fine-tuning/practicing your pitch,

5 x Y

20/20/20

it becomes *much* easier during the last 20 minutes to get them above the buying line quickly and close while they are truly at an all-time excitement high.

Another reason to employ the 20/20/20 sale: When you start a call knowing you are going to be pitching soon, you don't stay in the moment as well. You can start to cloud your early thoughts or make yourself nervous enough for it to come across in your tone if you have "closing" on your mind. By only listening and taking notes during the first 20 minutes, all of those thoughts subside and you can truly focus on listening and digging deep.

Conveniently, you also now have 20 minutes to think about and practice your pitch before you give it. Plus, if someone is 100 percent not going to buy, they will typically tell you not to bother calling back to pitch anyways! Just their saying, "Yes, call me back in 20 minutes—I am excited to see what you come up with" usually means they are closable.

The Five Yes Technique

Whether you decide to do a one- or two-call close, the way you use the Five Yes Technique is the same. Here is what it looks like:

1. Earlier you said X when I asked you Y. Is that true?
2. Earlier you said X when I asked you Y. Is that true?
3. Earlier you said X when I asked you Y. Is that true?
4. Earlier you said X when I asked you Y. Is that true?
5. Finally, earlier you said X when I asked you Y. Is that true?

I am certainly oversimplifying this for effect, but not by much. You literally read them back five of the digging deep questions and their answers and then ask them to agree that that is indeed the case.

This is why digging deep was so important and why I told you to write down what they said earlier. We are placing their answers to those digging deep questions into our Five Yes script.

Here is an example of a mortgage officer using the Five Yes Technique:

1. Earlier you told me your current loan amount is $330,000. Is that right?
2. Earlier you said your current interest rate is 5 percent. Is that right?
3. Earlier you said you're tired of paying so much each month to taxes and interest and so little to principal. Correct?
4. Earlier you said if I could save you at least $200 per month, working together would make sense. Remember?
5. Finally, you said your actual goal was not so much to save money on your mortgage as it was to start putting more money away for your kids' college funds. Is that how you plan to use the savings if we get this loan approved?

As you can see I reiterated a bunch of the logical questions, but also worked some more emotional ones in toward the end. You always want one of your Yes questions to be that they said they would move forward if it made sense. And you always want to make your fifth Yes their #1 emotional reason for buying. That's *why* you dig deep. Now they have to say no to their word *and* to saving money for their kids' college funds, not to me.

Be sure you are writing down your Five Yeses as you go along on a one-call close. Another benefit of doing a two-call close is that you can flip your script over to the back and literally write out the Five Yeses that you will use on them and what your Feature/Benefit/Tie Downs (covered in the next chapter) will be. There are way too many salespeople who think they are too cool for a script or to jot down a quick game plan before they pitch. Grow up. If you want to make big money annually in sales, you have to be willing to do the small things daily.

Our ultimate goal is a "*Yes*, I want to buy what you sell." But to get there most frequently, just before you start your pitch, use the Five Yes Technique. You will be amazed at how it shifts the power and momentum over to your side when it really matters, as you are about to start your pitch.

Chapter 13

How to Pitch Using the "Feature, Benefit, Tie-Down Technique" and Identify Exactly When to Close

Everyone sells features. The best salespeople sell features and benefits, and then tie down. Features are what you do. Benefits are why it matters to the lead. Tie-downs ensure the lead agrees throughout the pitch that the various features benefit them.

As an example, I would say on a call to start my pitch, "Curaytor is going to set up and maintain Facebook ads for you (Feature). By doing this a steady flow of hot new leads that include names, phone numbers, and email addresses will be in your inbox each day, ready for you to close them (Benefit). Does that sound like something that would help your business (Tie-Down)?"

Then I would do it again, using another FBT. "Curaytor is also going to build you a world-class website, landing pages, and blog (Feature) that we will use as the bait in the Facebook ads we run for you (it is always nice to tie the modules together when appropriate). Your clients, friends, and peers are going to tell you how much they love it and send you more referrals (Benefit), plus the people who check you out online before they contact you will be pre-sold (Benefit). Is that the kind of a web presence you are looking for (Tie-Down)?"

Pro tip: You can also use Fear blended into your Feature, Benefit, Tie-Down modules when appropriate. This is where you would purposefully point out a negative thing they are experiencing right now, in addition to the positive features of them buying what you sell. Identifying

F+B+T = C

and pouncing on their fears and pain points are often quicker paths to a sale than bells and whistles could ever be. Adding fear makes the sale about healing, not helping, which for many is the buying button that needs to be pressed the hardest. Instead of saying, "Do you want the best website in your industry?" I might say, "Would a website like ours help you fell less embarrassed when people check you out online?"

The template that could be used for FBT for any business is simple: "Here is what we do. Here is how what we do benefits you. Do you agree that there is a benefit in what we do?" Just ask yourself two simple questions. What makes my business great? What makes my business unique? The answers to those questions is where your FBT material should stem from.

By the way, of all the things I've covered, let me again remind you of the importance of tone. Particularly that yours should be full of enthusiasm (*I am sold myself*) during your pitch.

But there is really no need to overthink this. If what you sell is great, there should be several features you can point out during your pitch. I find that four to six well-thought-out FBTs (all of which you can script and practice in advance) seem to accomplish my goal of getting them more excited about buying than the cost. Which allows me to proceed to the next step: closing them.

This simple yet highly effective and proven sales formula is rarely being executed, and even when it is, it is not being done consciously or properly. When you compare someone who only pitches features, "Curaytor is going to set up and maintain Facebook ads for you (Feature)." to someone who pitches features AND benefits, "Curaytor is going to set up and maintain Facebook ads for you (Feature). By doing this a steady flow of hot new leads that include names, phone numbers, and email addresses will be in your inbox each day, ready for you to close them (Benefit)." the difference is crystal clear.

We actually use F, B, and T in our day-to-day lives a lot without knowing it, especially if you have children! I constantly use FBTs on my daughter Maya, who can be a challenge sometimes to get to do things without being asked several times.

Here is how you can even use FBTs on your kids: "Maya, I need you to clean your room (Feature) right now. Cleaning your room will give you more space to play and make it smell better, thus making your friends want to come over (Benefit). Will it be clean when I come back to check in 10 minutes so that we can invite Sofia over (Tie-Down)?"

ALWAYS BE CLOSING

The easiest way to remember FBT is to just think of it as the literal incarnation of the famous and oft-used sales quip from David Mamet's *Glengarry Glen Ross*, "Always Be Closing." With each module of FBT you complete, you are closing *during* your pitch, as opposed to just one big close at the end. These "minicloses" force the lead to agree that they need and want what you sell before you ask them to buy it with your "real close" at the end. If you are only talking features (and even benefits), but you are not using a tie-down, you will be *amazed* at how well they work, empowering you and giving you a clear psychological advantage over your caller.

As you proceed through your Features, Benefits, and Tie-Downs during your perfect pitch, there will be a moment when the person's excitement is higher than the cost of what you sell. Identifying this moment is critical.

This is why I never forgot this chart. When you're great at inside sales, you are laser-focused at getting to this moment at all times. With each module of Feature, Benefit, Tie-Down, we're taking them up the equivalent of one stair. With some people, you have to climb five stairs to close them. For some, it is only three. For others, it's seven.

Prepare the most compelling seven to eight Feature, Benefit, Tie-Downs you can come up with. But what we're really looking to do is to place one strategically in the middle that is our highest-valued item.

At Curaytor, we don't just run through the FBTs of our technology and strategies. We also know a big part of why we get hired is because we do all the setup for our clients. We set up their Facebook ads, their

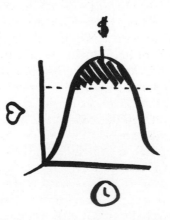

Figure 13.1

website and landing pages, their CRM, their monthly email marketing campaigns, and so forth. While we could certainly lead with this,
instead it's the land mine we place at the end that is more likely than
not going to be the stair that gets them over the buying line.

Save a juicy module for your final FBT. We get them excited about
the Facebook ads, the leads that will be coming in, the marketing that
will take place ... And now, the "final" feature is that we do it for you!
Benefit is that *you* don't even have to do any grunt work—by hiring
Curaytor you can spend your time on the moneymaking activities
that you enjoy. You get to keep your focus on people, while we focus
on your pixels and passwords. Tie-Down: Does that sound like the kind
of partnership you are looking for? *"Yes!"*

That's the moment we close.

Some people only need two FBTs. Some people will close themselves after the very first FBT. Sometimes, I will show one of our
prospects our websites to start my pitch and they're 100% sold. I can
feel their energy over the phone (mostly through the tone in their
voice). So it is a-okay to 100 percent abandon the rest of your FBTs
and close, if you are 100 percent certain they are above that buying
line after just one or two. Just say, "Great! So, here's what happens
next."

Sometimes you'll get to the moment that works almost every time
and you'll know in your gut that they're not ready. You can probably
tell from their tone (remember: tone is 55 percent of How Humans
Communicate).

The reality is that while you are trying to build a framework that
creates that moment like clockwork, every lead is different so listen
intently to how they answer the tie-downs.

*Pro tip: Sandbag a few additional knockout features in case they are
not sold enough to buy after the first four or five. Don't save the worst two
things you do for when you need them the most! If they weren't impressed
enough by your BIG FEATURE to close them, you'll need to impress them
with something else. By the way, some people you'll never get that they
are ready to close feeling from, but it's still your job to eventually just
close them anyway.*

When the FBTs have worked properly, you will have the lead over
the buying line and they're officially ready to be closed! When you do
identify that moment, here's exactly what to say. . . .

Chapter 14

Exactly What to Say When You Start to Close

Before I tell you exactly what to say to start your close, I want to tell you what *not* to say. Because I hear salespeople all over the country saying it and it's *killing* their production.

The biggest mistake in sales when closing a lead is the following statement: "So what do you think?"

I also often hear "How does that sound?"

Asking this type of a "How'd I do?" question in no way helps you sell more effectively. I get why you do it: Humans are insecure by nature and need to hear someone tell them they did a good job, that they liked what they heard. But that is not what a professional salesperson does.

Here is another quip I never forgot from my sales coach at FashionRock: The lion doesn't ask the lamb for food.

You don't ask them for their feedback after you pitch. If you followed all the steps in The Conversion Code sales call so far, *you know your pitch was great*. There is no reason to ask someone who doesn't do this for a living how you did. If you want feedback on your pitch, get it from your coaches and colleagues, not your customers.

If there's one thing you can and should 100 percent script and use every single time, it is your transition to a closing statement. You do not want to fumble at this critical juncture. It's the fourth quarter. You are on the one-yard line. Don't get cute.

Now that you know what *not* to say, here's exactly what to say when you recognize that it is the perfect moment to close:

"Great! So, here's what happens next ..."

If every time you pitch for the rest of your life, you say, "Great! So, here's what happens next ..." instead of "So, what do you think?" you will increase your closing rate instantly and dramatically.

Remember, you are using this transitioning closing statement as you complete your final Feature, Benefit, Tie-Down. As soon as they agree to the last tie-down, you immediately say verbatim, "Great! So, here's what happens next . . ."

Then you quickly foreshadow the next steps of what working together looks like by recapping what you are going to do to solve their problem and then clearly stating the cost and terms of them making a purchase: "Great! So, here's what happens next . . . Our company's going to do A, B, and C for you, which accomplishes your goals of X, Y, and Z. The price is X and the terms are Y. Again, we are going to do A, B, and C and the price is X." Don't be afraid to reiterate the offer, price, and terms. Just be sure when you do there is NO trepidation in your voice, or they will pick up on it.

It's closing time! Now that you have smoothly transitioned out of your pitch and started your, close it is officially time to ask the lead for their business.

Chapter

15

The Two-Step Close

You never want to get to the end of a well-thought-out call and then blow it at the finish line. This is payday. That is why I also make sure I use a proven script when I close.

To start closing, you are going to use what is known as the trial close. This is a question that isn't as scary as "credit or debit" or "yes or no," but it does force the lead to visualize that things are proceeding without you having to hard close them. Here is an example of the first step, the trial close, in action.

STEP 1: THE TRIAL CLOSE

Remember, we started our close with, "Great! So, here's what happens next ... Our company's going to do A, B, and C for you, which accomplishes your goals of X, Y, and Z. The price is X and the terms are Y. Again, we are going to do A, B, and C and the price is X." Now you are going to trial close by asking something like "Did you want to use your work or personal email address for our records?" When I sold loans, I would say, "Is a weekday or the weekend better for the appraiser to come out?" A real estate agent might say, "Are you going to want to look at houses during the day or early evenings?" At Curaytor I say, "What day of the week would be best for your first coaching call?"

With each of these examples, my goal is to get the lead to visualize that they are moving forward without having to directly ask them for their business. By doing this, they will typically either (a) answer your question, confirming that they are prime to be closed immediately using the next step (the slot close) or (b) ask a buying question or give you an objection before they answer. These are both good outcomes. Even if it is an objection, you are much better off trying to ARC (a technique you will learn in the next chapter) now than you are when you are really closing. If you ask for someone's credit card or commitment to work together and they object, it's awkward no

TC

matter how smooth you are. You want to use a trial close to uncover any last objections before you go in for the jugular, using the slot close to finish them off.

STEP 2: THE SLOT CLOSE

The second that they answer your trial close question, you really close by giving them two more choices. This time, though, both answers they can give are actually going to be a "yes" and you are going to be closing them. You literally want to say as soon as they finish their sentence answering your trial close, "Okay, great. And did you want to use a credit or debit card for the payment?" or "Okay, great. Did you want to use a business or personal card for the payment?"

I'm not sure exactly why, but it is much easier for people to make a choice like credit or debit/business or personal in the heat of that moment than it is for them to answer, "So, are you in?" or "So, are we moving forward?"

I often hear salespeople who normally never stutter start to when they ask someone for their credit card number. That shakiness in your voice and tone can be instantly identified by the caller on the other end. Sadly, everything you have done up until this moment can be thrown away by simply lacking the confidence to sound like you have done this over and over before. Remember, the lion doesn't ask the lamb for food. So don't act like a lamb when you ask for payment. If you do, the lead becomes the lion and you become dinner.

Here is how a professional salesperson asks for a credit card number: "Please read me the 16 digits on your card from left to right, 4 at a time."

Then after each block of four make sure you even add an "okay" so they know you are keeping up and writing it down. Act like an expert and you just might become one. Obsess that your words are coming out confidently and clearly when you close. For some, it helps to record their own calls and listen to them back to see if there is any trepidation in their voice. Personally, I use the TapeACall Pro mobile app, which lets me record both sides of a call from my cell phone with one click. Anytime you do this, I would highly recommend

SC

quickly mentioning that "Our call is being recorded for training purposes ..." to cover yourself and leave zero ambiguity around what you are doing and why. By recording your sales calls (with permission) and playing them back while you take notes, you aren't doing anything illegal—you're improving.

Sometimes depending on what you sell when you are "closing" you are not actually asking for payment, rather asking to meet in person. If that is the case, you still want to use a slot close after a trial close. The only change to the script would be replacing the previous example with, "So would you like to meet at 2 P.M. or 3 P.M. tomorrow?" or "Can I stop by on Saturday or Sunday to wrap this up?"

No matter how you define a close, using the trial close and slot close techniques back-to-back can boost your confidence and skyrocket your sales. There are a lot of times during this call where you get to go off script and make it your own. *When you are closing is not one of those times.*

By the way, as soon as they say, "debit" or "personal," don't be a rookie and lose your cool. It is funny how often the second a salesperson gets a credit card number they immediately "hit and run." This person just gave you their credit card number or commitment to work with you. Don't hang up the second they do. Especially after having just spent a good amount of time on the phone with them up to this point. In Chapter 17 I will actually teach you what to say when they say yes and how it can increase your retention and show rate dramatically.

The ugly truth is, no matter how good you get at closing Internet leads over the phone you will still hear "no" a lot. When you do, the key is to be prepared for it and do what you will learn in the next chapter, a technique called ARCing.

Chapter

16

What to Say When Someone Still Says No

Let's be honest. Even the best salespeople in the world hear "no" often. You can capture Internet leads, schedule quality appointments, and crush your calls, but you will never close 100 percent of your prospects. So in this chapter I will teach you what to say when they say no. The best thing about executing The Conversion Code properly is that you will hear no a lot less than you ever have!

BUYING QUESTIONS VERSUS OBJECTIONS

"I appreciate your time, but I'm not interested." That's a no.

"How long does this take? How does the billing work? Can I do X if I change my mind?" Those aren't no's. Those are called buying questions. If you did your job properly, people will have started to visualize themselves as a customer (which is exactly what we want), and when they do that, their questions quickly change from discovery to mastery. You flipped a switch in their mind that caused them to go from a brick wall mind-set to a buying one.

So when you close and it's not an explicit *yes*, remember that doesn't mean it's a no, either. Sometimes we take those buying questions for objections in the heat of the moment, when really it's just a logistical concern. In fact, it's great to get buying questions. And when you get them, you must remember to ARC.

ARCING

Similar to an ARP, an ARC also starts with Acknowledging the question they asked and then Responding (AR). The difference is that now the last letter, C, stands for Close, not Pivot. The way that you ARC is the same way that you ARP.

ARC

Here is an example of using an ARC when you get a buying question when you close:

ME: "Credit or debit?"
THEM: "How much is this going to cost me?"
ME: Acknowledge = "How much is this going to cost you? Great question."
Respond = "We charge A, which gets you B, with C terms. Doing this accomplishes the goals you told me of X, Y, and Z."
Close = "So did you want to use a credit or debit card?"

Short, sweet, strategic. That is what you want to focus on when you answer buying questions. Far too often, salespeople get a buying question and go into a long monologue to answer it, mistaking it for an objection. Rookie move. You already spent so much time up to this point with them on the phone. Trust the process. When you get a buying question at the end of your call, just ARC.

Think of the close like the fourth quarter of a big game. It's okay to be nervous, but you can't fumble when it matters most. This is why coaches spend a ton of time diagramming and practicing late-game situations with their players and why Michael Jordan took all of his game-winning shots in his mind well before he took them on the court. When the lights go on and the game is real, they are settled and confident, knowing they have a clear, scripted plan of action. You need to feel the same level of confidence when you're making your close.

Pro tip: Be sure to make a list of the most common buying questions you get (How long will this take to set up? How does the contract work? What happens if I decide to cancel?, etc.) and develop an ARC that works every time for each. Once you nail the ARCs that work the best, ride them until the wheels fall off.

Using ARC to Overcome Objections

You probably already know the objections you get the most as a salesperson. So get ready for what to say back by using proven ARCs that work. You don't need to reinvent the wheel—just develop and then lean on your go-to ARCs.

Here is an example of using an ARC when you close and get the spousal objection:

ME: "So to get started I need you to read your credit card number to me, four digits at a time."

THEM: "I need to talk to my wife first."

ME: **Acknowledge** = "You want to talk to your wife first? I can appreciate that. I always talk to my wife before making big decisions, too."

Respond = "Were you and your wife on the same page before we started this call? Do you think if we bothered her at work and conference called her right now, she would be okay with us accomplishing your goals of X, Y, and Z?"

Close = "Great! Then we will get the paperwork over to her, too. All I need to do that is for you to read me your credit card number from left to right, four digits at a time."

Here is an example of an ARC when you get the "I want to wait" objection:

ME: "So to get started I need you to read your credit card number to me, four digits at a time."

THEM: "I need to wait and think it over."

ME: **Acknowledge** = "You want to talk to wait and think it over? I can appreciate that. I do the same thing."

Respond = "Let's say we could time travel to 30 days from today— would accomplishing your goals of X, Y, and Z change? Sometimes indecision is the worst decision!"

Close = "If your goals will be the same a month from now? Then please read me your credit card number from left to right so we can accomplish them and wrap this up."

Here is an example of an ARC when you get a cost objection:

ME: "So to get started I need you to read your credit card number to me, four digits at a time."

THEM: "I like what you sell. But it is not in my budget at this time."

ME: **Acknowledge** = "Our price is too high for you? Sorry you feel that way. That usually means I actually didn't do a good enough job explaining everything that is included."

Respond = "Let's take a step back. When I asked you earlier, you told me that your goals were A, B, and C and that if we did X, Y, and Z, it would make sense to work together. While I can respect that price is an issue for you, there is also a cost to not taking action today. You don't accomplish your goals!"

Close = "I've really enjoyed speaking with you and I know you are making the right decision. Let's wrap this up. Did you want to use a credit or debit card?"

While you can predict and prepare for your most common objections, inevitably there will be a few you cannot foresee. I've actually gotten to the end of a *great* call, only to have the lead tell me that "I need to pray about this first." That's a very tough objection to overcome without being a dick. That is why you have to lean on your skills like ARC. Even when someone throws you a curve ball, you can at least still take a solid swing at it.

Here is an example of an ARC when you get an outside-the-box objection:

ME: "So to get started I need you to read your credit card number to me, four digits at a time."

THEM: "Sorry Chris, but I need to pray about this first."

ME: Acknowledge = "You want to pray about this first? I can appreciate that. I've prayed before buying something, too."

Respond = "Let me ask you. Have you ever prayed about this before today? If you were to put me on hold and pray right now (which I seriously don't mind if you do, if that would make you feel better), do you think whoever you pray to would want you to accomplish your goals of X, Y, and Z?"

Close = "Then let's wrap this up. Did you want to use a credit or debit card to move forward?"

I am not suggesting that using these ARCs will work every single time. But once you master them they do work more times than not. And they *really* help you separate smokescreen objections from genuine ones. The reality is that it can be difficult to overcome objections, but the other reality is that most of the objections you hear day after day in sales are basically the same. *Be prepared for them.*

Nail these ARCs. Call their bluff. How you handle these micro moments throughout the call, and especially during the close, is what will elevate you from a good salesperson to a great one.

Still a No? Using Preferred Additional Outcomes to Get a "Yes" Anyway

You can do everything we talked about in this book and you'll still get told no. That's the job. Even if you use the best ARCs (sometimes you have to ARC and re-close several times), the reality is there are some conversations that don't end in a deal.

When that happens, you need to immediately shift your focus to what I call "preferred additional outcomes." These are the things you would deem a success if a sale is impossible.

One preferred additional outcome could be to call them back the same day to see if they're in. This is for people who need to talk to their wife, to pray, or to think about it, and simply can't be sold on your call.

A second preferred additional outcome is a next-day callback.

A third (less appealing) preferred additional outcome is to send them some additional information by email and then follow up with them in a week/month/year based on their temperature.

It's okay to have a preferred additional outcome be email follow up, but certainly don't lead with that one. Lead with calling them back the same day or the next day. Remember earlier I referenced the quote, "Time destroys all things." Keep it mind here too when you schedule your follow-up call. The sooner it happens the better.

Even when I get a no and I deserved a yes, I get a yes. They say, "Yes, you can call me back later today." That's almost as good as a sale. They're *close*. Tomorrow? That's still pretty good too.

And what about if you say, "Can I call you back later today?" and they say no? Well, then, how about tomorrow? If that's a no, too, then it's obviously time to take a step back. Would you mind if I sent you some additional information about my company, what we do, and then follow up with you (in a week, six months, a year)?

I don't want to burn the leads that I got this far with because we did have a good, memorable conversation. I dug deep. I built rapport. I've got notes on them. When you are calling someone back later that day, the next day, or even six months later, you need to remember everything about them. So put it into your CRM immediately. Then follow up if they ever open your lead nurture emails or if they visit your website like I taught you in Section Two. You can hyperpersonalize the first minute of the next call 10 times more than you did this one, because you already will know so much about them.

Pro tip: Salespeople should move on as quickly as possible when they're told no because having a positive mental attitude is so important to getting the next yes. To expedite this, I have an email template that is prewritten because I don't want to write "Hey, thanks again for your time, I know we didn't . . ." in an email over and over. Have that template prewritten in Yesware or a Google Doc so you can send it very quickly.

Remember: Having a positive mental attitude and a black Lab mentality are a must. It sucks when you get told no, but you've got to bounce back quickly to be an elite sales performer. Thankfully, when you use my sales script and the conversation framework I've given you in this book you will hear yes more often than you hear no.

They Said Yes! Now What Do You Say?

Congrats, you made the sale. You cracked The Conversion Code! Now finish the call strong so they don't back out before you get paid. "Hit and run" selling is when a salesperson makes a sale and then within a second or two says, "Okay, thanks, bye" or "Okay, great. I will be in touch. Good-bye."

It's a rookie move that we make in the heat of the moment, and it is easily avoided with a simple script. As soon as someone finishes reading you their payment information, you are going to say exactly what you said when you identified the *exact* moment to close in Chapter 13: "Great. So, here's what happens next." But instead of foreshadowing the next steps in buying like you did last time, this time you are going to foreshadow the next steps in being a customer. Like, "Now I am going to get you over everything you bought, plus some additional information you will find useful that we send our new customers. Then, this is going to happen. Then finally, that happens. Got it? Good!"

In all seriousness, come up with exactly what you want to say after they say yes. You will be hearing it a lot more now!

Many commissioned sales jobs have what is called a "claw back," where they take money back out of a future check if someone cancels after they buy. There is no worse feeling in sales than having your commission taken back. By foreshadowing the next steps in the process as soon as they buy, you can do your part in reducing churn and keeping cancellations down. And if your "sale" is that you are meeting them in person, foreshadowing the process this one last time can help to increase your show rate at appointments.

I even take this post-sale tactic a step further by having an amazing email template (I use Yesware for Gmail for this) ready to send them as soon as we hang up. I call it "Thanks." It has some helpful additional details and online articles about what they just bought, and it thanks them again for their time and for buying from me.

I once read a story about Lewis Howes, who was selling $1,000 online training products and sending those who bought them a $10 brownie bites bag. He said that those bags reduced cancellations.

I don't send brownies, but I do use Bond.co to send a "handwritten" note to every lead I have a meaningful conversation with or that I close. The note arrives a few days later and thanks them for their time while letting them know I am looking forward to working together. The only thing I usually change on these is the first name and the address that I send it to, which takes only a second. I also make sure I include my cell phone number and email address below where I "sign" my name.

Be as strategic about your sales sticking as you are about making them in the first place. Besides, you just had an amazing call with this person and you are getting paid because of them. They said yes after you dug deep and used emotional buying reasons against them without their even knowing. The least you could do is tell them you enjoyed the date (call) before you close the door (hang up the phone).

Now that you know how to capture and close Internet leads, I'm going to teach you how to turn those closed sales into even more, free leads.

Chapter 18

How to Turn a Closed Internet Lead into Even More Sales

It takes real work to capture and close Internet leads. So you want to make sure that all of your effort creates more easier-to-convert leads in the form of referrals from your existing and past clients.

As I am sure you can guess by this point in the book, I do not leave this up to chance. I have developed a simple system for asking for referrals from current (or past) clients at the exact right moment.

A net promoter score (NPS) is a customer loyalty metric that is calculated by asking a simple question: On a scale of 1 to 10, how likely are you to refer us to a friend or colleague? What the research has shown is that 9s and 10s are "promoters" of your brand. Sevens and eights are "passive," and anything six or less is a "detractor." The survey also usually allows for them to give one additional answer: Why?

I make it a habit to send out NPS surveys two to four times a year to all our current and past clients. When I do, immediately afterwards, I segment the responses by 9s and 10s and I give that list of our "happiest" current and past customers back to the salesperson who originally closed them.

The person who closed them then follows up with a phone call to "check in" and see how things are going. Then after they speak to them we send them a handwritten note (using Bond.co), thanking them for their loyalty and business.

At the end of the strategically timed check-in call (and in a p.s. in the note we mail) we simply ask them if there is "anyone else who you know who we can also help." Boom.

If they are willing to give you a name or two (which they usually are—we knew they loved us before we called), try to also get the referral's email address and phone number. As soon as you do, let your scheduler do their job and follow up to book you an appointment (or you can call and book it yourself if you are the scheduler and the salesperson).

One mistake I see salespeople make day after day is not treating a referral lead the same as an Internet lead. Meaning, you must *always* take it from the top and use *all* the steps in the call. Don't skip building trust just because you think they trust you as a referral from a friend. The only difference between a sales call with a referral and an Internet lead is that you should use that information in your hyper-personalized opening: "Hey, John, I was speaking with Susie Smith and she mentioned that you might be interested in hearing about what we do at Curaytor. We've really helped Susie grow her business and would love to see if we can do the same for you!"

Then you do everything else exactly as you would with a web lead. Everything. Gain control, dig deep, Feature/Benefit/Tie-Down ... the whole experience. Don't cut any corners when working referral leads and remember that no matter where or how someone may learn about you, every lead is now an Internet lead and will check you out online either pre- or post-call before buying. So always take it from the top!

You can also generate a ton of referrals from your closed Internet leads by simply staying in touch with them through email and Facebook, post-sale. When you are doing what you learned in this book regarding email marketing, Facebook ads, and retargeting, you will have plenty of chances to stay top of mind long-term in a unique and meaningful way.

It is such a great feeling as a business owner to be able to send a helpful email or to run a genuinely useful Facebook ad to a new blog post I wrote that does not even try to make sales, but close a few anyways. I have hundreds of replies in my inbox that go something like this, "Awesome tips, Chris! Thanks. I wanted to introduce you to so and so. I told them they had to check out the work you are doing."

Once you get good, get greedy.

Capturing Internet leads, creating quality appointments, and closing more sales, as you have hopefully learned in this book, requires art and science. Speed and tenacity. Heart and heartless-ness....

But the one thing that cracking The Conversion Code does not require is luck.

Dan Gilbert, who I mentioned I worked for in the introduction and who is the founder of Quicken Loans and the owner of the Cleveland Cavs, said something once that I never forgot.

I will leave you with what he said; I often close out my keynote speeches at conferences with it. Keep it in mind as you now go off on your personal crusade to crack The Conversion Code:

"Innovation is rewarded, but execution is worshipped."

Nothing in this book works if you don't

If after reading and executing on what you learned in *The Conversion Code*, your business improves and you start capturing and closing more Internet leads, please send me a quick email (Chris@Curaytor.com) with specific details!

Bonus: Checking the Analytics and Metrics That Actually Matter (and what to do based on what you find)

O ne of the best things about digital marketing is the analytics and metrics it provides. One of the worst things about digital marketing is the analytics and metrics it provides.

When I was with Quicken Loans, one of the sayings that really stuck with me and has also resonated for the audiences I keynote for is "Innovation is rewarded, execution is worshipped." So much so that I even ended this book with the quip, hoping it would resonate with you as we part ways.

When it comes to The Conversion Code, execution is worshipped. The devil is not in the details. The devil is in not executing.

There are two things that matter significantly more than any digital metric I check—my gut and my growth. This simple G^2 mind-set guides my decisions much more so than page views, cost per click, cost per lead, cost per acquisition, click-through rate, reach, conversion rate, or open rate ever will.

G^2 is simple. Do you feel like what you are doing online is working (gut)? Is your profit increasing (growth)? When the answers are yes and yes, pour more gas on the fire.

Internet lead generation and conversion comprise several moving parts, like a website, landing pages, SEO, social media, email marketing, marketing automation campaigns, CRM, and SMS, to name a few.

Each of these moving parts comes with its own set of analytics and metrics you could check. In fact, more frequently companies are using machine learning or are hiring people called "data analysts" or "data scientists," and their entire purpose is to look at data and make recommendations based on what they find. The sad reality about digital marketing data is that it can really be spun in a way that makes it sound like things are great even when they are not.

Don't let all the social media gurus fool you. The best thing Facebook and the Internet in general enable is not "building a community" or "engaging your fans." It is building your business and bottom line. You do that by executing what you learned in this book.

I once did an audit of the Facebook advertising ROI for a top-10 mortgage company. I had their CEO send me the latest report they got each month from the high-dollar social media agency they had hired. My immediate reaction was that it must have been prepared by someone who really wanted to keep their job. It was all smoke and mirrors! As a salesperson first and foremost, I need leads to call—ideally, lots of them. So the number of and the cost per lead matters. Big time.

As I looked through the report I was nauseated by the focus on reach, engagement, new Likes, and popular posts. I would love to see you try to take those things down to the bank and deposit them. When I finally found the part of the report that addressed the number of leads generated and cost per lead. Their lead volume and conversion rate were terribly low, and their cost per lead was at least 10 times higher than it should have been.

To put that into a perspective that gets me excited about optimizing my marketing campaigns and looking at the metrics that matter, they could have gone from 150 leads a month to 1,500 leads a month, with the exact same ad spend, had they used The Conversion Code. What they were doing was passive. What I taught you is purposeful.

To keep you from wasting all of your time on pixels when you are better off focusing on people, I have put together a list of the analytics and metrics that actually matter and what you should change (or not change) based on what you find. Many of these metrics will be familiar to you just in name alone. Like in Google Analytics, "Time on Site" or "Page Views per Visit" is pretty straightforward, as are metrics like "Reach" or "Frequency" in Facebook Insights.

The gold in this bonus chapter is as much in what I am *not* including as it is in what I am. While you could certainly argue that I am leaving out something critical, for me, the following is *more* than enough to check and try to improve.

We started with websites and landing pages in Chapter 1, so let's start with those here as well.

WEBSITE METRICS THAT MATTER

Total # of and cost per unique visitor: You can easily calculate your total ad spend each month. You also want to know how many unique people visited your site during that same time period. This gives you a quick way to calculate your true cost per unique visitor. Total Ad Spend ÷ Unique Visitors = Cost per Unique Visitor. If you are getting a lot of "free" traffic through email, blogging, social media, or SEO, this will certainly lower the cost dramatically.

Total # of leads: How many leads did your website generate during the month? Be sure you are using a unique email address and a unique phone number on your website so that you can also track those who bypass the contact form and reach out another way. I do include new blog subscribers as website leads. While many of these are not ready to transact now, they will be later as long as you do what I taught you in Section Two.

Conversion rate: It is important to have a baseline for how your site converts traffic. By knowing this, you can feel much better about sending paid traffic there and spending more time on SEO. As an example, if my website is converting at 3 percent with the various calls to action I have in place, I know that if I drive 10,000 visitors a month, I will get a minimum of 300 leads.

Keep in mind that The Conversion Code taught you landing pages are > websites for paid traffic for this exact reason. Landing page conversion rates can be 10 times higher than a website conversion rate thanks to their one-page, one-purpose focus. However, the leads that convert through your website will often be of higher quality, even though they are a lower quantity when compared to landing pages. More on landing page metrics that matter ahead.

New versus returning visitors: With a well-designed website, content that is optimized for search engines and social media, a blog with a solid FAQ, and a fool-proof email follow-up system in place, your website will get a lot of new traffic, but be sure to also keep an eye on the returning traffic. Often someone will visit your website more than once, even a few dozen times, before becoming a lead. I like to make sure that at least 25 percent of my website traffic each month is returning, not new. The cost of getting people back to your website is a fraction of the cost of getting them there for the first time.

Page views per visit: If your page views per visitor are too low, it is very difficult to capture any leads. When you share a link to a piece of great content on Facebook, the most natural next steps for that visitor will be to leave, read something else related to what they just read, or to visit your home page. When they click through to your home page, they will have a plethora of additional ways to register or go deeper into what you do. This is why we spent so much time in Chapter One obsessing about our site's design! Bring them with content—wow them with your brand.

Average time on site: Similarly to page views per visit, if your average time on site is too low, it is also very difficult to capture any leads. Many of the "trapdoors" we placed on your site are dependent upon them visiting certain pages, taking certain paths, or spending a certain amount of time before they are triggered. It is hard to build trust to the point where someone would contact you and work with you if your average time on-site is thirty one seconds.

There are exceptions to this rule. Maybe your site is 100 percent focused on linking someone to a landing page. If that is the case, the lower the time on-site the better, potentially. But for most websites, if you want live chat, pop-ups, lead magnets, and contact forms to work, you need people to stay for a few minutes. I also like to look at my content and sort it by the highest time on-site average. You would be amazed at how bringing your visitor in using one piece of content can cause them to stay for 10 minutes and another may cause them to leave after 10 seconds. By identifying my highest time on-site pieces of content I can advertise more effectively and get more bang for my buck when I buy traffic.

Top-performing pages: I am constantly looking at what our top-performing pages and blog posts are. This is the easiest way to identify new content we should create. I also want to make sure that the pages and posts that get the most traffic are the most optimized for social sharing and search, and with lead magnets for lead generation. One thing you can do right now that will pay itself back again and again is to go into your Google Analytics and look for your top 10 pieces of content or pages of all time. Spend a few minutes on each one, "reoptimizing" them with the tips you got in this book. You must identify your HTPs (highest-traffic pages) and continue making them better and creating more like them.

Traffic sources: Direct (when someone types your URL into the browser), social (traffic from social media sites), organic search (SEO), referral (like from your email newsletter or another website linking to you), and paid search (SEM) are all easy to find and monitor in Google Analytics. Most of these are straightforward. Your goal is to be fairly diverse. You don't want all your eggs in one basket. As an example, even if to start your traffic is all coming from Facebook, your direct traffic should increase as your brand gets out there more often and your referring traffic should go up as you follow up with emails that link back to you.

One pro tip that I even see many professional marketers miss is tracking their mass emails or social media campaigns as hyper-specific referring sources of traffic in Google Analytics. This can easily be done by using Google's URL Builder form. Not only can you do this for email marketing or Facebook ads, but also you can do this to better uniquely name and track ANY online campaign that you run involving a link.

$$G^2$$

Doing this makes it very easy to better identify how a specific campaign performed. You will find that certain types of content lead to a much deeper and longer visit than others. Not only will you know how many total people and total page views a campaign created, but also you can see what the average length of the visit was compared to par for your site's overall traffic.

I find that my email newsletter campaigns with links back to my site are some of the best-performing links for time on site and page views per visit.

Top exit pages: When you optimize your site and content like I covered in Chapters 1, 2, and 3 you will have a plethora of outbound links that go to other websites and also to your lead magnets/landing pages. While you may think that your top exit pages are a bad thing, when looked at through The Conversion Code lens they are a good thing. Remember, landing pages always convert better than websites, so it can be a win to understand which pages the most people are exiting from. This can be a good indicator that you best optimized those pages with the right links and calls to action!

Paid search results: One thing that every company should do is at least run an SEM/PPC campaign in Google for your own brand or name when it is searched. When you buy an ad for what someone was literally searching for, it gets clicked a lot. With an ad in Google versus just relying on the organic result, we get much more control over what is displayed and the calls to action. Paying for this, and any other keywords you may be advertising in Google, can become costly, so it is imperative that you look at your analytics for the results of those campaigns.

LANDING PAGE METRICS THAT MATTER

Total number of visitors: When you spend money on Facebook ads or time on optimizing your website and your content with lead magnets to get people to your landing pages, you want to make sure all that work is paying off. Building landing pages is not enough—you must purposefully drive traffic to them each and every month without fail using the tactics you learned in this book. Most companies are keeping track only of the number of visits to their primary website. You need to keep track of that *and* the number of visitors to your landing pages.

Total number of leads and the cost per lead: Using a CRM integration or even a simple spreadsheet, you need to track the total number of leads from your landing pages each month. You also want to divide that by the money you spent to get the traffic to them. This gives you your true cost per lead.

Conversion rate: Now that you have your number of visitors and your total number of leads, you have your conversion rate. Landing pages can literally convert anywhere between 0 to 100 percent based on a number of factors. And you also have to be careful to simply look for the highest conversion rate possible. Many times for me, a landing page that converts at 6 percent nets my company more revenue and growth and actual paying customers than a landing page that converts at 70 percent. Why? The amount of information you collect on your landing page will certainly impact your conversion rate. But, again, you have to find a balance because the more you collect the better you will empower your sales team when they call.

This is when I apply a G^2 mind-set. If a landing page is working, it means that sales and marketing all agree that we are getting good leads from it and growing because of it. If I know in my gut something is working, regardless of how the data may compare or juxtapose with "baselines," I don't overanalyze.

Traffic sources: Sometimes the best thing that your website does is send people to your lead magnets/landing pages. If the foregoing website metrics are poor, but your website is a *huge* referral source to your landing pages, which are capturing leads that are converting into sales, you are in a great position. This is why G^2 matters with all metrics. If you are growing and you know things are clicking, it would be very scary and naive to make landing page changes that marginally improve cost or quantity of leads, even if the metrics are "ugly" on the surface. Just like with your website and its traffic sources, be aware of what the best sources of traffic are to your landing pages. As with your website, where 10 percent of your content may end up getting you 90 percent of your page views, 10 percent of your landing pages might end up getting you 90 percent of your leads. Once you find and launch one that works, ride it until the wheels fall off and don't get too cute. Just focus on getting what works in front of more people.

You want the traffic to your landing pages and lead magnets to rival that of your website. Sure, you will most certainly get *way* more page views, visitors, and time on-site using a traditional website and blog. But those things will not convert leads at nearly the rate your landing pages will. As an example, if we got 100,000 page views in a month on Curaytor.com, I would want to also get *at least* 25,000 page views on our landing pages during the same period.

FACEBOOK METRICS THAT MATTER

Link clicks: The majority of our focus on Facebook is driving traffic back to our website and landing pages using links. So I keep a close eye on how many link clicks each ad I run gets. If an ad is only getting good reach, but not a lot of clicks, I bail.

Click-through rate: The average click–through rate in the United States in Q1 of 2015 was .84%.[1] By doing what I taught you in this book you should be closer to 2–5%. I have even had Facebook ads get higher than a 10% click-through rate. A good rule of thumb would be to try to be between 1.5–3%. Under 1% is not ideal. Over 2.5% is strong.

Reach: To get the volume of clicks I need, I also have to factor in the reach of the ads I run. If you want hundreds of clicks and leads you can't target 2,000 people. Think of reach like this: If you target your ads at the size of a large university (or larger), they will get a lot of action. If you target your ads at the size of a large high school, they won't. There will be times when you want to reach a small number of "perfect" clients. Just keep in mind that when you do the volume of clicks and leads won't be there so the quality better be.

Impressions: When you run as many Facebook ads as I do the impressions can really add up. While I normally don't get excited about impressions, they do have tremendous value for me in one undeniable way. I am EVERYWHERE online in the eye of the lead and I hear time and time again that "I saw your stuff following me around." Your goal for total impressions should be the number of people you want to reach times the number of times you want to reach them each. You can be better off having 100,000 people see your ad 10 times each versus having 1,000,000 people see it once.

Relevance score: Facebook now grades each ad that you run on a scale of 1–10. While they have not disclosed everything that goes into their scoring system, be rest assured that their underlying goal of the score is to identify quality versus crappy ads. Google uses a similar approach when scoring how PPC campaigns are performing. The better the score the better the ad. The better the score the better your future ads will be placed and positioned. Also, a high score usually means that you got a high level of engagement which leads to Facebook showing the ad to more people for free, organically.

Frequency: While I do want to reach a lot of people several times each with my ads, I don't want the frequency at which they see them to get too high. If someone has seen my ad 30+ times and still has not engaged, I would rather stop that ad and come up with another angle that might work. I also try not to kill an ad until it has been seen at least a handful of times minimum. You cannot expect your ad to be seen only once and get everyone who will click it to click it the first time they see it.

Per AdEspresso, "the more the frequency (of a Facebook ad) increased, the more the CTR decreased and the average Cost Per Click increased. The numbers don't lie, at a frequency of 9 the average cost per click increased by 161% compared to the beginning of the campaign."[2] So as frequency increases so does cost per acquisition. Bottom line? Frequency really matters so keep an eye on it.

Most popular posts: I am constantly using my Facebook page's Insights tab to identify my top performing posts. As my #1 purpose on Facebook is link clicks, I sort all my old posts so the ones with the most clicks all time are right at the top. Then I spend a few minutes figuring out why and planning to run more ads like the best ones I find.

EMAIL MARKETING METRICS THAT MATTER

When it comes to my email campaigns I look at a few specific metrics. As important as emails are to The Conversion Code, you will want to keep an eye on how the ones you send perform. The obvious and most important email metric will be the size of your list and making sure it is always growing.

When I look at my email marketing data I focus on open rate, click-through rate, reply rate, and the percentage of those who unsubscribed. Most systems today do not track how many people reply automatically the way they do opens, clicks, and unsubscribes. But if the replies go to you, you can search your inbox by "re: subject line" and calculate them manually. Opens and clicks are great, and solid indicators that we should call a lead as I discussed in Section Two, but replies are what get conversations started, and conversations create closes.

If you search "email open and click-through rates by industry," you can get a good baseline to work against if you have no idea what is "good" is for your vertical.

My email list currently averages greater than 30 percent open rates, greater than 3 percent click-through rates and a less than 1 percent unsubscribe rate, for some context. But I can also, anytime I need or want to, get those numbers up to over 50 percent and

10 percent by (a) being very clever with my subject line and calls to action or (b) segmenting my list down so that what I send them is more relevant than something I might send to everyone.

By the way, do not let unsubscribes discourage you in any way. Your email list having some churn is healthy as long as it is not too high and you are always adding new leads to it. Plus, we want to send emails to people who want to buy, not people who want to bitch.

Don't forget that you need to check these metrics for your mass emails but also your drip emails. I am amazed at how few companies make changes and improvements, based on hard data, to their monthly and drip email campaigns. Small tweaks can net large results with email copy. We once asked through email for leads to "Tell us about your current home's condition," which did get some strong replies. But by changing it to "On a scale of 1 to 10, how would you rate the current condition of your home?" we removed some friction and dramatically increased the reply rate, even though at the heart of our message was basically the same exact question.

I also find it useful to look more closely at which links got the most clicks when there is an email with multiple calls to action. Your first link will almost always get the most clicks no matter what you do, but I also find takeaways in seeing the volume of clicks for each specific link that was an option. This helps me keep an eye on what resonates, or not, with my list and leads. If a link farther down gets more clicks than several above it I immediately take note.

Lastly, I go back once a quarter to see what email subject lines performed the best for getting opens and clicks. This gives me clarity around what my next quarter's messages should focus on. Great subject lines for emails are just as important as great titles are for blog posts.

SALES METRICS THAT MATTER

Total number of sales. That's it.

Like my first sales coach told me, "There is only enough room on my spreadsheet at the end of each month for results, not excuses, intentionally."

Sure, number of leads called, number of leads received, number of appointments scheduled, show rate, close rate, total talk time logged, and hours worked can all be good metrics to watch and will certainly have a direct correlation with results. But only results matter. Make sure you are paying your marketer, scheduler, and closer, based on closed deals, not vanity metrics that don't actually drive the bottom line.

I am also a fan of "feeding the fat," meaning that your top paid salesperson should always make more than the CEO does (minus any crazy bonuses or stock options they may get). For example, if I paid myself as the owner of Curaytor $150,000 a year, I better also have a clear compensation plan for my top-performing sales reps that makes them $150,001.

If you look at the cover of this book, after an arguably complex journey to get to where you have indeed cracked The Conversion Code, all that is at the bottom of my funnel diagram is a $. That is because the entire purpose of The Conversion Code is to put a laser focus on making more money by using the Internet and all of the innovations that have recently occurred in the worlds of marketing and sales.

Again, there are other metrics that matter that I am not including here on purpose. I am sure I will even get a few nasty emails, especially from marketers, saying that I have really oversimplified this section. I don't care. My G^2 matters more than any argument (however valid) they could make.

I hope by sharing my personal journey as specifically as I could that I've inspired you to take your marketing, sales, lead generation, and lead conversion efforts to heights you didn't even know existed. There were so many people who taught and inspired me along the way. It only felt right to teach and inspire others in return.

I'd love to hear how executing The Conversion Code works for you. Please email (Chris@Curaytor.com), message me on Facebook (FB.com/CuraytorChris), or tweet me (@Chris_Smth) with any specific results you get from reading the book and doing the work. Please use #TheConversionCode when you do.

Also, please pass this book along to any marketer or salesperson who you think it can help (preferably ones at *huge* companies who should bring me in to teach them The Conversion Code and coach their sales and marketing teams).

You must have foreseen a well-timed call to action to close out the book, right?

Notes

HOW TO CRACK THE CONVERSION CODE

1. 8 Seconds to Capture Attention: Silverpop's Landing Page Report. Report. 2009. Accessed September 30, 2015. http://www.silverpop .com/downloads/white-papers/Silverpop-LandingPageReport-Study.pdf.

CHAPTER 1

1. Pamela Briggs, Elizabeth Sillence, Lesley Fishwick, Peter Richard Harris, "Trust and mistrust of online health sites" (paper presented at the Conference on Human Factors in Computing Systems, Vienna, Austria, April 24-29, 2004). http://www.researchgate.net/ publication/221516871_Trust_and_mistrust_of_online_health_ sites

2. Code Academy. "Reimagining CodeAcademy.com: Our 10 Design Principles." Code Academy https://medium.com/about-codecademy/reimagining-codecademy-com-1ebd994e2c08

3. U.S. Department of Health & Human Services. http://www .usability.gov/

4. Anderson, Myles. "Local Consumer Review Survey 2014." https:// www.brightlocal.com/2014/07/01/local-consumer-review-survey-2014/#internet BrightLocal. 1 July 2014.

5. Kovash, Ken. "Changing the Firefox Download Button." https:// blog.mozilla.org/metrics/2008/11/21/changing-the-firefox-download-button/ Mozilla Blog of Metrics. 21 Nov. 2008.

6. MarketingSherpa. *Landing Page Handbook*.

CHAPTER 2

1. Hubspot State of Inbound 2014–2015.

2. Hubspot State of Inbound 2013–2014.

3. Lee, Kevan. Buffer. "The Anatomy of a Perfect Blog Post: The Data on Headlines, Length, Images and More." 28 May 2014. https://blog .bufferapp.com/perfect-blog-post-research-data

4. Turnbull, Alex. "The Power of Storytelling: How We Got 300% More People to Read Our Content." 22 April 2014. https://blog.bufferapp .com/power-of-story

5. PR Web Blog Stat.

6. Wei, Jiyan. "Increasing Time-on-Page Through Aesthetics (Lessons Learned from PRWeb and Build Zoom - Two Large Content Sites)" PRWeb & Buildoom Studies. https://moz.com/ugc/increasing -timeonpage-through-aesthetics-lessons-learned-from-prweb-and -buildzoom-two-large-content-sites

7. Lee, Kevan. Buffer. "The Ideal Length of Everything Online According to Science." https://blog.bufferapp.com/the-ideal-length-of- everything-online-according-to-science 31 March 2014.

8. Opt-In Monster. "50 Blog Post Ideas That You Can Write About Today." http://optinmonster.com/50-blog-post-ideas-that-you- can-write-about-today/

CHAPTER 3

1. Ryan Deiss. July 9, 2014. Digital Marketer. http://www .digitalmarketer.com/lead-magnet-ideas-funnel/

2. Software Advice & Adobe. *Social Media Content Optimization Survey*. http://b2b-marketing-mentor.softwareadvice.com/the-social- media-content-optimization-survey-1013/

3. BrightEdge Whitepaper. *Social-Share Analysis: Tracking Social Adoption and Trends*. April 2013.

4. Patel, Neil. *QuickSprout*. "The Ultimate SEO Checklist." http://www.quicksprout.com/2015/01/19/the-ultimate-seo-checklist-25-questions-to-ask-yourself-before-your-next-post/ 19 Jan. 2015

CHAPTER 4

1. Ingram, Matthew. "Facebook has taken over from Google as a traffic source for news." http://fortune.com/2015/08/18/facebook-google/ 18 Aug. 2015. *Fortune Magazine*.
2. Spencer, Jamie. "The Science of Posting on Social Media." http://www.setupablogtoday.com/the-science-of-posting-on-social-media-infographic/ Accessed 30 Sept. 2015

CHAPTER 5

1. Mailchimp. "Email Marketing Benchmarks." http://mailchimp.com/resources/research/email-marketing-benchmarks/
2. Retargeter Blog. "7 Best Practices for Running a Retargeting Campaign." https://retargeter.com/blog/strategy-2/7-best-practices-for-running-a-retargeting-campaign

CHAPTER 9

1. Hubspot. "All the Marketing Statistics You Need." http://www.hubspot.com/marketing-statistics-1

BONUS CHAPTER

1. Reiss-Davis, Zachary. "Salesforce Ads Benchmark: Key Trends Across Facebook, Twitter, LinkedIn." Salesforce. https://www.salesforce.com/blog/2015/07/salesforce-ads-benchmark-key-trends-across-facebook-twitter.html 8 July 2015.

2. AdEspresso. "Silent but deadly: The Frequency of your Facebook Ads." https://adespresso.com/academy/blog/facebook-ads-frequency/ 27 January 2015.

OTHER RECOMMENDED READING:

"Anatomy of a Perfect Landing Page." https://blog.kissmetrics.com/landing-page-design-infographic/

Jiyan Naghshineh Wei. The Impact of Multimedia on News Consumers.   http://www.cision.com/us/2010/04/the-impact-of-multimedia-on-news-consumers/

Index

Note: Page references in *italics* refer to figures.